PADRE PIO

IRISH ENCOUNTERS WITH THE SAINT

COLM KEANE

First published in Ireland in 2017

by

CAPEL ISLAND PRESS
Baile na nGall,
Ring, Dungarvan,
County Waterford,
Ireland

ISBN 978-0-9559133-9-6

Printed and bound by Clays Ltd, St Ives plc
Typesetting and cover design by Typeform Ltd

For Seán

Colm Keane has published 26 books, including six number one bestsellers, among them *Padre Pio: The Scent of Roses* and *Padre Pio: The Irish Connection.* He is a graduate of Trinity College, Dublin, and Georgetown University, Washington D.C. As a broadcaster, he received a Jacob's Award and a Glaxo Fellowship for European Science Writers. His books, spanning 13 chart bestsellers, include *Going Home, We'll Meet Again* and *Heading for the Light.*

CONTENTS

Love is the spark of God in the soul of man.

Padre Pio

INTRODUCTION

Padre Pio loved the Irish. He admired the depth of their faith, once remarking how 'Ireland is a country beloved by God.' His face would light up when introduced to people who had travelled so far to meet him. 'Ah, the Irish!' he would exclaim in Italian when discovering where they were from. He also took an interest in Irish Church affairs, supporting, for example, the building of a new basilica at Knock.

He counted among his personal friends people like John McCaffery, who lived in Donegal, Fr. P. Hamilton Pollock, who was based in Limerick, Donal Enright, from County Cork, Mairead Doyle, who lived in a house appropriately named 'Franpio' in Dublin, and others with strong Irish connections including the Irish-American heiress Mary Pyle. They were always welcome in his company; if they were men, they were welcome in his cell.

The Capuchin friars around him also loved Ireland. Fr. Eusebio, who was Padre Pio's assistant from 1960 – 1965, came to Ireland to study English. So, too, did Fr. Alessio, who assisted him for six years and knew him well. Yet another assistant, Fr. Ermelindo, learned his English in Donegal and Cork. 'I feel in Ireland like at home,' Fr. Eusebio once said. 'I find the Irish people very like the Italian people, warm and friendly as they are.'

Each of these assistants brought with them to Ireland extraordinary, intimate stories about their stigmatised fellow friar. Take, for example, Fr. Alessio, who described how he had once seen the stigmata: 'They were horrible to look at. I had always wished to see them, but once I saw them, I prayed, "God, don't ever let me see them again." His hands were like those of a leper, they were so corroded.' He had also slept in a cell next to Padre Pio's and was aware of the friar's many battles with devils. 'Once I would be there, he wouldn't be scared,' he recalled.

Fr. Alessio said he knew if sick people who came seeking cures would live or die. 'I know from experience,' he remarked, 'that when Padre Pio said to the sick person, "I'll pray for you" or "Let's pray to God," the sick person was going to be healed. On the other hand, if he said, "Let's resign ourselves to the will of God" or said nothing at all, the grace of healing was not to be.'

The warm, intimate relationship between Padre Pio and his fellow friars, on the one hand, and the padre's Irish devotees, on the other hand, was not only unusual but quite profound. In the pages ahead you will see how close that relationship was from the accounts of early pilgrims who travelled by boat and train and walked up the dusty road to the friary. You will also read the stories of so many others who arrived at a later stage on comfortable package tours from Dublin and Belfast.

You will additionally become acquainted with miracles and cures, not to mention the friar's saintly aroma, ability to bilocate and to read people's minds. These traits and characteristics will feature prominently throughout the book. In the meantime, we need to familiarise ourselves with the extraordinary mystic of San Giovanni, starting with what happened in September 1918 when five deep lesions appeared on his body – the stigmata or five wounds of Christ.

On Friday, 20 September 1918, Padre Pio sat in the choir loft of the friary chapel at San Giovanni Rotondo saying prayers of thanksgiving after Mass. It was between nine and ten o'clock in the morning. He was alone. The normal darkness of the chapel seemed even duskier in the early autumn light. Everything was deathly quiet. He was, he later said, overcome by a sense of peacefulness 'similar to a deep sleep.'

Mayhem suddenly broke loose. The crucifix in the choir loft transformed itself into an 'exalted being' whose hands, feet and side dripped blood. The friar was terrified. Beams of light and shafts of flame burst forth from the being, wounding him in the hands and feet. 'What I felt at that moment is indescribable,' Padre Pio later recalled. 'I thought I would die.' The being then disappeared, not a word having been said, leaving Padre Pio lying on the floor, his hands and feet oozing blood. A wound in his side, which had appeared at an earlier date, was also bleeding.

Padre Pio was aged 31 when the 'visible stigmata' appeared on his body. There had been evidence of stigmatic marks in the past, but they had proved transitory. He had also experienced what are referred to as 'invisible stigmata', where there was pain in all the relevant body parts but no bleeding wounds had appeared. Although the earlier stigmatic manifestations had caused great discomfort, nothing compared to the physical pain and shame he felt after the events of September 1918.

'I am dying of pain because of the wounds,' he wrote, 'and because of the resulting embarrassment which I feel deep within my soul. Will Jesus who is so good grant me this grace? Will he at least relieve me of the embarrassment which these outward signs cost me?' Despite his plea, the wounds – and the pain – would remain with Padre Pio for almost exactly 50 years, up to his death in September 1968.

At first, news of Padre Pio's stigmata travelled slowly, by word of mouth. Soon, everyone in the village of San Giovanni knew. Nearby villages were next. After that, reports spread like a raging fire, with the established Italian press hot on the scent of the latest gossip by the spring of 1919. Suddenly, to his discomfort, the humble friar, from a modest, unassuming, peasant family in the tiny village of Pietrelcina, was an overnight star.

People flocked to the friary at San Giovanni to get a glimpse of this extraordinary man. They crammed into his Masses, queued for interminable hours to attend his confessions, and waited by doors or in corridors to receive his blessing or to touch his robes. Women, in particular, were drawn to him, arriving each morning to seek his absolution at confession or to beg his intercession over family concerns.

Soon, there were rumblings about miracles and cures. A blind man was said to have recovered his sight after being blessed by Padre Pio. A soldier's gangrenous foot was healed even though doctors declared it to be untreatable. The lame cast off their crutches and walked. Tumours disappeared from those with cancer.

Strange, sweet perfumes emanated from the blood of his wounds. He appeared at the bedsides of the sick in their homes while simultaneously being witnessed by his colleagues back at the friary. Those attending his confessions were shocked when he read their souls, recounting sins only they could have known.

The local secular clergy were annoyed. Their congregations started deserting them, preferring instead to attend Mass and confession at the friary. More damagingly, money contributions were drying up and being redirected to the friars. The local Archbishop of Manfredonia, Pasquale Gagliardi, was furious. His complaints to Rome would soon have a telling effect.

Gagliardi bombarded the pope and many other ecclesiastical authorities with allegations that Padre Pio perfumed himself, wore makeup, was involved with women and that his confessions were a disgrace. The friar, he said, was 'demon-possessed.' Later it would emerge that Gagliardi might more accurately have been referring to himself. Not only was he accused of sexual immorality and neglect of duty, but he was also denounced for selling valuable church property to line his pockets.

Mud sticks, however, and Padre Pio paid a heavy price for the archbishop's scurrilous inventions. He was debarred from saying public Masses or from hearing lay confessions, prohibited from revealing the wounds or speaking about them, prevented from corresponding or interacting with devotees, and a decision was taken to move him from San Giovanni to a friary where he might disappear from view.

All these measures were implemented, breaking Padre Pio's heart, with one exception – his planned relocation. It was rescinded after a massive public protest involving 5,000 infuriated locals. They were determined not to lose their beloved friar, and they succeeded, ensuring that Padre Pio remained in San Giovanni up to the day of his death.

Separated from his spiritual children, Padre Pio accepted his fate and obeyed Rome's commands. His pastoral duties removed, he was effectively a prisoner in the friary at San Giovanni. He prayed, said Mass in private and lived the life of a simple priest. He was 46 years of age before things changed and he was once more restored to his public ministry.

There would still be little peace for Padre Pio in the decades ahead. He was continually investigated by the Vatican, whose emissaries beat a well-worn path to San Giovanni enquiring into his case. Further restrictions were imposed, all of which he obeyed. It wasn't until 1963 – while in his mid-70s – that he was granted complete freedom by Pope Paul VI, who features later in this book.

His health was always precarious, to say the very least. He suffered from asthma, bronchitis, chronic gastritis, a painful kidney stone, arthritis in later age, and even had a malignant tumour removed from his ear. He slept little – just a few hours each night – and ate less. His diet was insufficient to maintain him, a doctor concluded. His body, he said, was like good soil, requiring little nourishment to support it; hence his robust appearance.

His wounds continually caused pain and discomfort. They never became infected and never healed, even though other scratches and everyday lacerations healed quickly. He lost a cupful of blood through the wounds each day, adding to the pressure on his body. His body temperature was startling, registering up to 118 degrees Fahrenheit even when well. This latter phenomenon he shared with other stigmatics.

He worked prodigiously, undertaking tasks his fellow friars would never contemplate never mind complete. Rising at 3.30 a.m., he would prepare for his daily Mass, which he celebrated at five a.m. He spent up to eight hours hearing confessions each day. He engaged with his visitors and devotees, dealt with sacks of letters, and still had time to oversee the building of a state-of-the-art hospital in San Giovanni. The rest of the day he spent in contemplation and prayer.

It was surprising he lived as long as he did, to the age of 81. His final years were difficult. He was feeble and clearly in pain. He could barely shuffle onto the altar to say Mass. His memory was fading. Worn out from a tough life, with its complications and controversies, it was clear from just past the mid-1960s that the end wasn't far away.

In 1967, the stigmata started fading. The first to go were the feet, followed by the side. Next, the stigmata on the hands began to fade and by summer only dried crusts and a pink redness remained. Padre Pio was beginning his journey home to heaven, and he knew it. He would finally reach there on 23 September 1968.

THE EARLY YEARS

1918 – 1949

Ireland was blighted by political upheaval and economic stagnation in the first half of the twentieth century. There were two world wars, a civil war, a trade war with Britain and a worldwide depression to contend with. Jobs were scarce, money was tight and foreign travel was unknown. The prospects of taking a trip to Italy to see Padre Pio were slim.

Many Irish-Americans had the resources to undertake the journey. So, too, did international luminaries with Irish links. Irish priests, with their Rome connections, and soldiers who fought with the Allies during World War II also travelled. Add in an assortment of curious writers and you are left with a trail of disparate figures heading off to meet Padre Pio.

Dublin-born Dr. Paschal Robinson was almost certainly the first Irish person to meet Padre Pio. He did so in the 1920s, having been asked by the Vatican to investigate the friar.

The news coming from the tiny village of San Giovanni Rotondo in the Gargano Mountains was of great concern to the Vatican. They could hardly believe the information they were receiving. Stories of a stigmatised friar who could read people's minds, bilocate and bring about miracles and cures were bad enough;

worse were reports of hysterical crowds flocking to his Masses and confessional.

Even in those early days, the 1920s, they did what any powerful organisation would do today – they decided to send one of their sharpest troubleshooters to find out what was going on. They selected a man who was fast becoming a highly-regarded Vatican diplomat – the Dublin-born Franciscan by the name of Dr. Paschal Robinson. He set out on what was, in effect, a secret mission to discover what was happening and to report back to his superiors in Rome.

By that time, Dr. Paschal Robinson had already written two books on the stigmatic St. Francis, one book on St. Clare, and another on the Franciscan order. He was clearly talented, having worked as a well-regarded foreign correspondent for American newspapers in the UK, and then – after becoming a Franciscan – teaching at university level in the USA. Nobody was more qualified to carry out this delicate, discreet task than Robinson.

Paschal Robinson was born in Dublin's Herbert Street in 1870. He was christened David at birth but he would later take Paschal as his Franciscan name. His father, a journalist, was well-regarded in Dublin literary circles. However, in 1875 – little more than 20 years after the ending of the Great Famine – Robinson's parents decided to depart for America, taking their five-year-old son with them. No one would have guessed that in 1930 – 55 years later – the young boy would return as the Vatican's Papal Nuncio to Ireland.

We can see from Robinson's early career how he was selected to conduct an investigation of Padre Pio. Having received his

Doctorate in Sacred Theology, his rise was stellar – publishing four influential books in the next eight years and being appointed by no less than the pope as Professor of Medieval History at The Catholic University in Washington D.C. Aware of his prolific talents, he was eventually inducted by the Vatican to its diplomatic service in Rome.

He arrived in Rome in 1919 and was soon on his way to the Peace Conference in Paris where settlement terms were being agreed by the Allies following the ending of World War I. He excelled himself in his initial diplomatic assignment, primarily representing Catholic interests in Palestine and Africa. Further diplomatic ventures followed, mainly in the Near East but also including a successful spell in Malta where he sorted out some thorny divisions between Church and State.

It was in the 1920s that Dr. Robinson made the long and dusty journey to San Giovanni Rotondo to investigate Padre Pio. He first examined the friar's wounds, concluding that the reported bleeding actually occurred and the wounds were real. This, alone, was significant as allegations had surfaced that the phenomenon was a hoax. His conclusion mirrored those of many other investigators at the time who despite variations in their observations reported coin-sized lesions, covered in a wide film of crusted blood, which would break into shards and dig into the friar's flesh, causing severe pain.

Some said the wounds were shallow; others reported that they were deep; another said that they fully pierced the hands so that light was visible through them. Most said the wound in Padre Pio's side was shaped like a cross. The majority noticed blood emanating from the lesions; at least one other saw no bleeding at the time of examination. Many were agreed that Padre Pio tried to cover them and was seemingly embarrassed by them. Dr. Paschal Robinson concurred, pointing out that the publicity associated with them was unsought by the friar.

It was also noted that Padre Pio felt palpable pain from the lesions, with one investigator, Dr. Festa, observing that the friar could not fully close his hand. Many remarked on the fragrance of the blood, with comments often made about how it smelled like perfume or 'the scent of roses'. As to why the wounds were there in the first place, and whether sheer mental concentration might be the cause, Padre Pio's answer was always the same, advising that the person who asked should go out into a field, concentrate as hard as possible on a bull, and see if horns start to appear on their head.

We do not know whether Dr. Robinson was impressed by the padre's reasoning or whether he believed that some other self-inflicted, medical, psychological or supernatural factors might explain the wounds. Like many churchmen, he seems to have avoided the issue. Other investigators reached their own conclusions – one, Dr. Festa, concluded that the wounds were definitely stigmatic and of supernatural origin; another, Dr. Bignami, argued that they were most likely the product of suggestion allied to the use of chemicals; a third, Dr. Romanelli, said that any speculation would be beyond the competence of a physician.

Dr. Robinson concluded that Padre Pio should not appear in public as long as the stigmata were present. This recommendation, echoed by other investigators, had significant consequences in subsequent years. At various times, the friar was banned from saying public Masses, hearing lay confessions, meeting with devotees, answering letters or revealing his stigmata in public. His public role restricted, he was effectively hidden away in the friary at San Giovanni. Eventually, these restrictions were rescinded.

The investigations of Dr. Robinson and others mentioned above would not be the only – and certainly not the last – that the Vatican would institute concerning Padre Pio. Over the years, they sent archbishops, monsignors, Holy Office prelates and regular priests, all acting as investigators; the Capuchin Order sent their investigators, too, including their Minister General. There was a notable procession of men in coloured robes and exotic hats making their way to report on this extraordinary friar and, more importantly, to determine what action the Church should take.

Many of their reports have been lost in the mists of time. Indeed, we might never have known of Dr. Paschal Robinson's investigation had it not been for a diplomat with the British Legation to the Holy See who revealed the details of Robinson's visit eight years after his death. The diplomat, Alec Randall, was not only an admirer and friend of the Irishman but he and his colleagues played an integral role in establishing diplomatic relations between the new Irish Free State and the Vatican.

The establishment of these diplomatic links resulted in the arrival, in 1930, of Dr. Robinson as the first Papal Nuncio to

Ireland since the seventeenth century. He served the role well, becoming a beloved, revered and well-known figure in Irish life, involving himself with charitable organisations and other Catholic action movements. The *Evening Herald* noted his 'courtesy and charm of manner' which firmly endeared him to those he met.

Dr. Robinson served as Papal Nuncio up to his death in August 1948, when he passed away at the Nunciature in the Phoenix Park. Although he died just a handful of miles from where he had grown up more than seven decades earlier, he had lived a full life in the interim and played a small but notable role in the story of an extraordinary friar living a long way away in the Gargano Mountains in Italy.

From the beginning, Padre Pio was known for his daily Mass. It became the hallmark of his life.

Words like desire, hunger, passion and yearning are inadequate to describe Padre Pio's love of the Mass. From the moment he said his first in 1910, in the appropriate setting of his home village of Pietrelcina, to his last 58 years later, in San Giovanni Rotondo, he lived and died for his Mass.

During Mass, the altar became Padre Pio's personal Calvary. His intensity was spellbinding. He sobbed and wept. He shook uncontrollably and was lost in communion with God. Pale and exhausted, he suffered intensely, his feet aching, his hands bleeding, his side throbbing, as he relived the death and resurrection of Jesus Christ. Once, when asked how he remained standing at the altar, he replied, 'In the same way as Jesus remained upright on the cross.'

Raising the chalice to the heavens, his sleeves would fall back and reveal his wounds. The congregation, already utterly spellbound, would gasp. It was the only time when they could witness the stigmatised hands; during the rest of the day they would remain bandaged. There was something intensely moving about what they were seeing – a stigmatised friar who bore the five wounds of Christ reliving the crucifixion of his master on the cross.

Perhaps Padre Pio best explained his love of the Mass. 'My heart beats very fast whenever I am with Jesus in the Blessed Sacrament,' he wrote to his spiritual director. 'It sometimes seems to me that it will leap out of my chest. Sometimes, at the altar, I feel as if my whole being were on fire; I cannot describe it to you. My face, especially, seems to want to go up in flames.'

Witnesses provided their observations, too. Among them was the prolific author and schoolteacher, Malachy Gerard Carroll, who, because of his Irish background, was familiar with the character and passions of his fellow countrymen, particularly their love of Padre Pio. Among his numerous books – which included a biography of Matt Talbot – he wrote one of the earliest works on the mystic of San Giovanni. Like almost everyone who witnessed the friar – and he did so by visiting him – he was particularly moved by his Mass.

'Perhaps it is safe to say that nowhere in our world is there another priest who celebrates Mass as though he were bearing

Christ's cross through every moment of it,' Carroll wrote. 'There is an expression of suffering on his face at the supreme moments of the Mass, and his body sometimes is seen to twitch with pain. His fingers tremble and hesitate about breaking the Host, as though the veil has been rent for him and the reality of what he is doing has become too intense.

'His lips shiver as he raises the Chalice. When he genuflects, it is as though an invisible cross has crushed him down, for he rises painfully and with the utmost difficulty. There are moments when he seems lost in colloquy with God, when he moves his head as though nodding assent and he speaks some abrupt words.

'Sometimes he weeps, as though a shadow of the world's sin has come between him and the Eucharistic Jesus. His compassion for the Christ he sees mocked again is great. And there are those hands exposed during the Mass, and otherwise hidden by the brown woollen mittens he constantly wears. Those hands can be seen, with the stigmata on them, the mystic shadow of the nails. And sometimes they bleed.....'

Carroll also observed the elongated, protracted, seemingly interminable pauses that characterised the stigmatic's Masses, during which he would appear lost in thought or, perhaps more correctly, deep in communion with a greater power. One such pause was especially noticeable during the memento of the living, where he prayed for the intentions of those who were still alive.

'In that deep silence, the congregation crowded behind him really feel that he is taking their lives, their worries, their ambitions, their sins and their sorrow for sins, all the spotted reality that is their human nature, with its heroisms, its groping, its cowardices, and is lifting them up to Christ in hands that are shadowed with Christ's wounds. It is a mighty moment for any man whose name is in the heart or on the lips of Padre Pio.'

Other pauses were noted by Carroll – one arising during the memento of the dead, when the faithful departed were prayed for; another arising during Padre Pio's communion, when he received the Eucharist. Above all, however, the final blessing marked perhaps the single most important moment of prolonged reflective silence for those in attendance. With the Mass over, Padre Pio faced the congregation, his hand raised, his sleeve sliding up his arm, and with the stigmata visible he issued his blessing.

'Every man sees a hand raised in blessing over him – a hand marked with a bloody wound,' Carroll concluded. 'Calvary becomes a reality, and the Mass appears in all its shattering wonder for each and all. It is impossible to have any more than a vague, groping questioning about the silence of Padre Pio as he stands transfixed on the altar.

'That silence keeps its secret. But of one thing we can be certain – this silence reaches out to the silence in the heart of each one kneeling there, and according to the depth of spiritual silence within each heart will the real message of Padre Pio be felt. The great, radiating meaning in the life of Padre Pio is his Mass.....'

The following is a spiritual love story from the early 1920s. It concerns Mary Pyle, an American heiress of Irish heritage, who gave up her privileged life to live alongside Padre Pio in San Giovanni Rotondo. She remained there for 45 years.

The year 1923 was a notable one in Europe for all the wrong reasons. In Germany, Adolf Hitler staged his Munich putsch; in Italy, Mussolini set up his Fascist Grand Council; in Ireland, the Civil War was still raging. In America, things were looking more cheerful – those were the Roaring Twenties, an era of prosperity, consumerism and innovation. Jazz was the rage; prohibition was on the wane; everything seemed possible.

Things were particularly pleasant if you were rich. The Rockefellers, Carnegies and Mellons were prosperous beyond anything ever known before. Other lesser-known dynasties were extraordinarily affluent, too. Among them was a family named McAlpin – they had dropped the 'e' at the end of the name some time before – which had direct Irish connections.

The patriarch of the family – James McAlpin – had emigrated from Ireland to America in 1811. He was accompanied by his wife, Jane. They had married in County Antrim in 1809, before departing on the *Jupiter* for a new life in New York.

Their son, David, made his fortune from the manufacture of tobacco. He also owned large chunks of real estate in Manhattan. David's son, in turn, constructed the Hotel McAlpin in New York, which at the time was the largest hotel in the world. Another son married a Rockefeller. By the 1920s, the

McAlpins were serious contenders among the upper end of America's extremely rich.

It was into this family that Mary Pyle was born in 1888. She was the daughter of Frances Adelaide McAlpin and James Tolman Pyle. Her father's family were affluent, too, and well-known as the founders of Pyle's Pearline Soap. Not surprisingly, her early life was privileged – the best schools, learning foreign languages, studying music and holidaying in Europe.

On one of those trips to Europe, Mary, aged 25, converted from Presbyterianism to Catholicism, with her baptism taking place in Spain. Her mother was distraught and disinherited her daughter from her will, although she later relented and reinstated her as a beneficiary. It was in Europe that Mary heard of a strange mystic in Italy named Padre Pio, and in 1923 she decided to pay him a visit.

The meeting between Pio and Pyle, by all accounts, had a profound sense of mystery and magic about it. She later described what happened: 'I fell on my knees and said, "Father." He put his wounded hands on my head and said to me, "My daughter, do not travel anymore. Stay here."' And stay there she did. She transferred what little wealth she had to the friary, joined the Third Order of Saint Francis – consisting of lay members living in the outside world – and donned the Capuchin habit and sandals which she wore for the rest of her life.

In the years that followed, Mary Pyle looked after the poor and sick in San Giovanni, taught young children their catechism and helped out with the choir. She also attended Padre Pio's Mass every day and, afterwards, would drop into the friary to help reply to his overseas mail – this latter task being made possible by her proficiency in many foreign languages. At the beginning, she must have seemed a strange figure in the village; eventually, however, people warmed to her presence and referred to her as 'L'Americana'.

It wasn't long before her mother – deeply concerned by her daughter's impoverished lifestyle – came to visit. A wonderful, if somewhat shocking, story is related about the mother's introduction to the friar. This somewhat sniffy woman, with her tiny dog at her feet, stood waiting in the sacristy for Padre Pio to arrive. Once the friar entered, the dog ran towards him and started barking, prompting the padre to kick the animal out of his way. Mary's mother departed in an indignant huff.

Later, the mother mellowed and established a very close relationship with Padre Pio. She also reinstated her daughter's monthly allowance, which was a handsome sum at the time. Mary used the money to build herself a house in San Giovanni, which became a centre point for overseas visitors and for the spiritually-inclined who wished to stay on a more permanent basis. With her mother's financial assistance, she also built a friary and seminary at Pietrelcina, and contributed to the building of a new church.

Mary's kindness extended to Padre Pio's parents who she looked after in the latter years of their lives. They stayed with her in her San Giovanni home, which the friar visited on the back of a mule because of the difficulty he had walking on his wounded feet. It was there, in Mary's home, that both parents eventually passed away.

Mary Pyle spent the remainder of her life in San Giovanni Rotondo, where she continued to be a committed follower of Padre Pio. Her life's work was dedicated to his cause; her loyalty irrevocable and almost unreal. She, more than anyone, believed he was a living saint. Of all the women who were drawn to him – and there were many – she was the one who really stood out.

It was no surprise, then, that Padre Pio was deeply moved when he heard in April 1968 that Mary had suffered a stroke and had been taken to hospital. With his health also failing at the time, he was unable to visit her. Nor could he attend her funeral after her death on 26 April, aged 80.

Looking back, it might be said that Mary Pyle was to Padre Pio what St. Clare was to the other stigmatic, St. Francis. There was a similar, indelible bond between them. In that context alone, it seems appropriate that, within five months of her death, Padre Pio also passed away, believing no doubt that he would meet her again along with the angels he hoped she would encounter on her arrival 'home to heaven,' as he put it.

Most Irish people first learned of Padre Pio through newspaper reports beginning in 1919 and stretching to the late 1940s.

On Tuesday, 3 June 1919, the *Evening Herald* brought to the Irish public the first newspaper account of strange goings-on in southern Italy. The paper, which was in existence since 1891, led its front page with the story 'Friar's Stigmata' and 'Strange

Cures Performed at San Giovanni.' It also featured the eye-catching, mysterious sub-headline 'Miraculous Gifts.'

The story, bought in from the *Daily Chronicle* – which was owned at the time by British Prime Minister Lloyd George – provided a remarkably accurate account of what was then known about Padre Pio. It detailed not only the appearance of the wounds but the friar's aroma of perfume – 'resembling that of the woodlands in springtime' – and his miraculous powers. Padre Pio, the correspondent wrote, 'of late years has gained widespread reputation and fame as a prophet, saint and wonder-worker.'

Irish readers would have undoubtedly been captivated by the page-one lead story in this popular newssheet. Their eyes would have been particularly drawn to the reference concerning miracles. The paper didn't let them down, recounting a story from a doctor from Barletta who described how a young patient of his had received a miraculous cure. She had previously been at death's door.

One morning, he arrived at the girl's bedside, only to discover that she was in perfect health. The girl recalled how, during the night, she had been visited by a bearded friar who had laid his hands on her, declared who he was, and left. Neither the patient nor doctor had ever heard of Padre Pio but the girl's friend had and had sought the friar's help for her friend's recovery. On visiting San Giovanni, the doctor was shocked to discover that the friar's appearance tallied precisely with the girl's description.

The *Evening Herald*'s front-page report on Padre Pio was not only the first to be carried in Ireland but was one of the first to appear anywhere in the world. His name and attributes had been mentioned in print for the very first time only a month before, in May 1919, in Italy's influential daily newspaper *Il Giornale d'Italia*. The following month, June 1919, *Il Tempo* revealed how he had healed a soldier whose gangrenous foot was deemed by doctors to be untreatable. This miracle was also mentioned in the *Evening Herald*'s story referred to above.

It took a year before Britain's *Daily Mail* was describing to its readers how people were flocking to San Giovanni to see this holy man. Their coverage, of course, was seen by their Irish readers. Further coverage continued throughout the 1920s, by the end of which the friar's story was red-hot reading for those anxious to know more about the twists and turns in his extraordinary life.

The Cork Examiner, in November 1929, brought news of concerns in Rome over the friar's activities and popularity. The newspaper reported how, having been ordered to Rome, the people of San Giovanni had prevented Padre Pio from doing so, fearing he would never be allowed to return. Instead, the newspaper recorded – accurately – how 'the Holy Office prohibited Padre Pio from writing, preaching, lecturing or from taking part in any activities of that nature.'

A few years later, in 1932, the *Kerry Champion* also tackled the restrictions on Padre Pio, revealing how books about him had been banned and placed on the Index. Using copy from *The Catholic Sun*, it reported how investigators found 'no evidence' that the stigmata were of supernatural origin – an assertion only true up to a point – and claimed that restrictions were imposed to 'guard the faithful from excess.' The truth of 'our religion', the article said, 'does not depend upon such extraordinary happenings, although, doubtless, they may serve to increase faith and devotion of a certain kind.'

Perhaps it was the return of Irish soldiers and airmen who had served with the Allied Forces during World War II that inspired the spiralling interest in the fortunes of Padre Pio among Irish people in the late 1940s. Reports that he was 'seriously ill' surfaced in 1949, resulting in a wide range of newspapers recording the event.

'Weeping villagers gathered outside the Capuchin monastery near Foggia, Southern Italy, last month when they heard that Padre Pio, who had the Stigmata since 1918, was seriously ill,' the *Derry People and Tirconaill News* reported on 26 November 1949.

It says something of how the friar's fame had spread that the same report was carried in the *Ulster Herald*, *Nenagh Guardian*, *Fermanagh Herald*, *Mayo News*, *Anglo-Celt* and *Strabane Chronicle*. The stage was set for the mass coverage the stigmatist would receive up to his death in September 1968 and, further on, to his beatification and canonisation.

Perhaps the most comprehensive coverage of the 1940s was provided by the *Longford Leader* in May 1947. Reprinting from *The Irish Catholic*, it reported some interesting facts about Padre Pio: how his five wounds bled night and day, while any other wounds he accidentally received had always healed naturally; how his body always had a temperature of at least

108 degrees Fahrenheit, enough to kill any ordinary man; how his chest wound was on his left side, while Christ's was on his right side. This latter matter Padre Pio dismissed by saying, 'Only Christ had His on the right side. We must bear ours on the left.'

The article concluded by stating how 'the Church makes no official pronouncement concerning Padre Pio's reported stigmata. Church policy dictates that no announcements are made in such cases until after death. Then all the circumstances are investigated and any legitimate sanctities officially pronounced.'

Although these were still early days, the *Longford Leader* and *The Irish Catholic* had quite clearly set out the process that would ultimately lead to the friar's beatification in 1999 and canonisation in 2002. Those events, however, were a long way away, and a lot of water was to pass under the bridge before then.

The pioneering educationalist Maria Montessori not only had a strong connection with Waterford, but her visit to Padre Pio in the 1920s also had an Irish link.

There was a minor revolution over the standard of children's education in Waterford in the early 1900s. A well-attended protest meeting was held in the City Hall in April 1909. People were dissatisfied with the quality of what was on offer in the city's schools. They wanted something different, something better for their boys and girls.

That 'something' was on the educational horizon already, but it wasn't in Waterford or even in Ireland. It was a new system of educating children devised by an Italian woman named Maria Montessori. From a wealthy family, she had studied medicine at the University of Rome, becoming Italy's first female doctor. From her early work with special needs children, she developed a new method of teaching that turned educational thinking on its head.

Montessori's approach was simple and successful. Children were no longer lectured to while fixed in their desks. Instead, they were given facilities for practical play and allowed develop at their own pace. They were no longer, as she put it, 'like butterflies transfixed with a pin,' but self-motivated, active little beavers, handling things and working out problems under the supervision of their teachers.

In Rome, in 1907, Dr. Montessori opened her first school dedicated to her methods. It was called Casa dei Bambini, or Children's House, and it was a great success. Her methods spread rapidly throughout Italy, Europe and the world. Children loved the new school environment and developed at a faster pace.

A Montessori course, to be held in London in 1919, caught the eye of one of the Waterford protesters. She attended and the rest is history – within a year, the first experimental Montessori class was established at the local St. Otteran's School, Philip Street, and later that year a full school, with certified teachers, was opened at Bishop Foy's.

Maria Montessori was delighted with the Waterford school initiatives. She visited the city to see for herself, first in 1927, and again ten years later, in 1937. On her 1927 visit to St. Otteran's, she was greeted by children holding a welcome banner made from pink roses. She was highly impressed with the standards she witnessed, as she stated in the visitors' book before departing, adding that she would never forget her brief time at the school. She was equally happy with her visit ten years later.

Maria Montessori always travelled with an interpreter and we are told that a 'Miss Cornish' interpreted for her at St. Otteran's in 1927. Had the visit taken place four or five years earlier, the person accompanying her would have been Mary Pyle – the Irish-American heiress who gave up her privileged life to live alongside Padre Pio in San Giovanni Rotondo and who featured earlier in this chapter.

What I didn't mention in the earlier section on Pyle was that, prior to her 1923 visit to Padre Pio, she had been the interpreter and close companion of Maria Montessori. They had travelled throughout Europe as a twosome, like mother and daughter, with Montessori spreading her new educational ideas far and wide and, because she was relatively poor at languages, relying on Pyle as her translator and interpreter. Without Mary Pyle, Maria Montessori's mission would have come to a juddering halt.

Montessori must have had a knot in her stomach when she heard about Mary Pyle's visit to San Giovanni Rotondo in 1923.

She knew that Pyle was not only intensely Catholic but also seeking something spiritually new. When she heard of the interaction between Pyle and the friar – with Pyle instantly dropping to her knees and the friar prompting her to stay in San Giovanni – she must have feared the worst.

As it happened, Pyle didn't immediately stay in San Giovanni. Instead, she returned to Capri, where Montessori was based, and told her what had taken place. She then asked Montessori to come with her to meet Padre Pio and witness for herself what a wonderful, holy man he was. This Montessori did.

We don't know what Montessori's reaction was to Padre Pio when they met in San Giovanni. What we can deduce, though, is her disappointment when Pyle told her she had decided to pledge her life to the friar. After their visit, the two women headed for the bus, with Pyle deciding to accompany her companion to Rome where she intended to collect her belongings. They never made the journey together. Instead, as they were about to board the bus, Pyle cried out that she felt she was nailed to the ground and couldn't leave. She remained in San Giovanni for the rest of her life.

Maria Montessori returned alone to Rome that day in 1923, after which she never spoke to Mary Pyle again. She felt crushed by what she regarded as her former companion's betrayal and, as far as she was concerned, the relationship was over and their friendship had come to an end. She never returned to San Giovanni, either, and it is said that she deeply resented Padre Pio for taking away her trusted friend. Hers was one of the few cases where someone who came to meet Padre Pio ended up aggrieved at the end of their visit.

Perhaps all this was mere history, and totally forgotten, by the time Maria Montessori made her two visits to Waterford in 1927 and 1937. The truth is, we don't know. We do know, however, that the Montessori concept soon spread to other Waterford schools and throughout the country. We also know that Montessori remained enamoured by what she frequently referred to as those 'beautiful Waterford schools' that had adopted her methods in the early 1920s – those pioneers of Irish education that she remembered up to her death in 1952.

From the early years, Padre Pio was treated by zealous admirers as a rock megastar might be treated today. Irish woman Stella Collins witnessed the phenomenon.

Within a year of the stigmata appearing, a sense of madness was in the air. Frenzied and passionate women flocked to the Capuchin monastery, desperate to see Padre Pio. Most of them were local. They wished to talk to him, touch him, discuss their problems with him or just be near him.

Padre Pio would walk from the friary to the chapel, only to encounter hordes of excited women blocking his way. Some would fall at his feet and grab his robes; they were summarily brushed aside by the friar. Many beseeched him for blessings; others cut snippets from his clothes as souvenirs. In time, he needed security to protect him from the frenzied mob.

There was chaos at his five a.m. Masses. Crowds of women milled at the chapel door. Once opened, they surged to the top pews, battling each other for the best vantage points. Strangers and visitors were shoved out of the way. Voices were raised and arguments ensued, with the result that Padre Pio would admonish them loudly, warning them to be quiet and to remember they were in the house of God.

There also was madness outside his confessional. Committed regulars believed they had pride of place in the queue and God forbid anyone who tried to dislodge them. Sometimes, newcomers were bumped out of their way. There were reports of people being kicked, knocked or generally manhandled. Some of the most troublesome offenders would try to interrupt the friar while his confessions were in train.

The worst and most determined of these overzealous women became known as the 'Pious Ladies'. In time, many of them believed they had special-access rights to their 'friend' Padre Pio. He tolerated them, although they annoyed him and wore him out. They also upset Pio's fellow friars, who had never seen anything like them before.

Nor had Stella Collins ever seen anything like them before she and her husband travelled from Dublin to San Giovanni Rotondo. Not only did the couple receive Padre Pio's blessing and kiss his hand, but they assisted at his Mass on four occasions. She also witnessed the chaos that erupted each morning.

Having risen at four a.m., she and her husband 'joined the milling throng,' Stella wrote in an article for the *Irish Independent* on her return home. 'Around 4.30 a.m. a tiny aperture was opened and the seething masses crushed and pushed amid the admonitions of the men and cries of women in the crowd.

'Eventually the door was thrown wide open and the swaying masses fell forward towards the church. We gained admittance as best we could and then all of us scampered to the Altar of Saint Francis at the right-hand side of the church. We found a chair, placed it in position and sat down with a sigh of relief.

'But our troubles had not ended. People behind pushed and pummelled until we felt our ribs would break. By the time we had accustomed ourselves to the crush from behind a "child" of twelve to fourteen years had got into an upright position on the chair directly in front of us and refused to be moved in spite of all entreaty.'

Contrary to what might be expected in a church, the noise often increased in volume as the time for Padre Pio's Mass approached. There was no settling down, no gradual onset of silence, no sense of the sacred nature of what lay ahead. Instead, in Stella Collins' experience, the Mass was awaited not 'with awe and reverence, but amid a din and tumult on all sides.' As five o'clock drew near, 'the hustle and bustle increased still more,' she remarked.

Soon, Padre Pio exited the sacristy and entered the church. His arrival at Masses was frequently greeted by cries from his fervent admirers of 'Santo,' 'Santo,' a reference to their belief that he was a living saint. He would turn to them in annoyance and ask them to be quiet. There were no cries concerning his saintliness at Stella's Mass, but there was enough commotion and chatter for the stigmatist to issue stern rebukes.

'Padre Pio's approach was heralded by one monk while another endeavoured to hold in check the rising emotions of the crowd,' according to Collins. 'At times Padre Pio reprimanded the mob himself as he prepared to celebrate Mass.

'Once during Benediction he had to order some women to kneel to make room for others. Then again his voice could be heard thundering "Leave the church" to two girls who had attempted to photograph him. I was reminded of Our Lord's just anger with the money-changers in the Temple.'

Everywhere at Mass, Collins noticed the many sorrows and sufferings of daily existence. A blind young man groped his way around, guided by the loving hand of his ageing mother. A deformed girl was led towards the altar rails. Collins also saw, and met, an eight year old girl who had suffered from birth with a serious heart problem. Her mother had begged Padre Pio to ask God if she might live for at least 12 years. The girl presented Stella with a photograph of her First Holy Communion, which she had received from the hands of Padre Pio.

Despite the pandemonium, for Stella Collins her visit to San Giovanni was one of wonder and joy. 'We Irish find it difficult to understand the Italian attitude to religion,' she said by way of dismissing the wild happenings she witnessed. Instead, the inconveniences were outweighed by seeing Padre Pio conversing with God and experiencing at the end of Mass his 'bleeding suffering hand' raised in blessing. 'What a contrast this presented to other holidays abroad,' she concluded, as her visit to the 'humble Capuchin friar' of San Giovanni came to an end.

One of Ireland's favourite entertainers in the first half of the twentieth century – the opera star Gigli – was a longstanding personal friend of Padre Pio.

From his initial visit to Ireland in 1934 to his last in 1954, Beniamino Gigli, who was one of the world's greatest-ever tenors and successor to Caruso, captivated Irish audiences. The reaction was similar to the excitement that greeted The Beatles in 1963, although not as boisterous. Packed houses, standing ovations, multiple encores and rave reviews characterised his shows.

Four thousand opera lovers were crammed into Dublin's Theatre Royal to witness the Italian superstar perform. Two thousand saw him at the Savoy in Cork. Belfast's Ulster Hall was stuffed to the gills. At one show, he was obliged to give 13 encores; at another he gave 12; at yet another show the audience were said to have 'brought down the house' after his rendition of an aria from Verdi's *Aida*.

The reviews were ecstatic. *The Irish Press* went into raptures, highlighting his 'beautiful' voice, his 'perfection,' his 'sincerity,' concluding that only one word could adequately describe him – 'magnificent!' The *Irish Independent* wrote of his voice being 'rich and pure in tone,' 'abounding in vitality' and 'scintillating in its brilliancy.'

He even hit the headlines for his kindness to an Irish fan – a Limerick newsboy named Frank Reidy, who not only collected Gigli recordings but who traded letters with the tenor. The two exchanged Christmas cards and other greetings each year. Gigli sent him an autographed photo one New Year's Day. He also invited him to London to hear him sing.

It was no surprise that Gigli was awarded an Irish 'Oscar' in 1950 – one of the prestigious statuettes that were being handed out at the time by the Catholic Stage Guild of Ireland. The award said a lot. Truly, the Irish loved him, and he loved them. He loved their music and musical appreciation, their sense of national identity, and he also was friendly with the Irish tenor John McCormack. If ever an international star became one of Ireland's 'own', it was Beniamino Gigli.

What was little known in Ireland at the time was the deep love and admiration Gigli had for a humble friar back in Italy by the name of Padre Pio. He would visit him as often as he could. He would sing one of his best-known songs, *Mamma*, at the friar's request. It always reminded the friar of his mother, Mamma Peppa, who had died in 1929. He had loved her so deeply that he would frequently walk away with tears in his eyes while Gigli was singing.

It seems hard to credit that a voice which, at the time, was thrilling packed venues like the Metropolitan Opera House in New York, La Scala in Milan, Covent Garden in London, never mind the Theatre Royal in Dublin, would also provide private, personal renditions of songs like *Mamma* for an isolated friar in an even more isolated outcrop of rock in southern Italy. Yet, up to his death, that's exactly what Gigli did.

Wonderful though their relationship became, it didn't start well. At the time of his first visit to San Giovanni Rotondo, he was already an international household name. Drawn there by tit-bits of information he had gathered from his friends, he was determined to meet the man of the moment – Padre Pio. We know about his arrival at the friary. Dressed to the nines in the finest clothing – he was always a stylish dresser – Gigli appeared in a top-of-the-range limousine, driven by a uniformed chauffeur, which no doubt stirred up much interest never mind a lot of dust!

Padre Pio was far from impressed. After staring at the star for a moment, penetrating his soul, he proceeded to ridicule his name, Gigli, which translates as that purest of flowers, the lily. Without pause, he accused Gigli of sullying his name by being involved in an adulterous relationship with another woman, behind his wife's back. He then picked on his first name, Beniamino, which translates as 'beloved'. Far from being beloved by God, the friar said, he was the opposite because of the parlous state of his soul.

It must have been a tense, dramatic moment, to say the least. Things could have gone either way. It would not be unrealistic to suggest that an international celebrity of the magnitude of Gigli might have turned on his heels, got back in his car, and returned to Rome. Instead, Gigli melted in the presence of the padre, who eventually became his confessor, and, according to accounts, quit his adulterous relationship and established a friendship with the friar that lasted up to the time of his death in 1957.

In the following years, Gigli undertook many visits to San Giovanni and became a regular contributor to Padre Pio's hospital fund. In fact, it is often said that he donated a portion of his substantial income to the building of the Casa Sollievo della Sofferenza, known in English as Home for the Relief of Suffering. More importantly, he developed a warm, personal friendship with the friar that was noted by those who saw them in each other's company.

Despite their respective claims to fame – and both were worldwide celebrities when they knew each other – the two men seemed to share something basic in common. It boiled down to the word simplicity. Beneath their popularity, they were both simple men. Just as Padre Pio had come from a poor background and was noted by his colleagues as 'a simple friar', so too did Gigli grow up in poverty, working as a milk boy to help his father – a cobbler – put food on the family table.

That simplicity – many referred to it as honest, unpretentious charm – was noted in Ireland, too. It may well explain how, quite apart from his extraordinary talent, he captured so many Irish hearts. It was especially singled out when Gigli died in November 1957. Writing in the *Sunday Independent*, James Delany remarked how when he first met the star he had expected to encounter a difficult and haughty man. Instead, he turned out to be the entire opposite. Just as with Padre Pio's death 11 years later, it may help us understand how, as Delany put it, Gigli ended up being loved everywhere and how the passing of this 'great son of Italy' was mourned the world over, including in Ireland.

Padre Pio's ability to be in two places at the same time became legendary during his early years as a friar. The following describes two examples of the phenomenon – one involving an Italian; the other one concerning an Irishman. Both people experienced not only his visits but also his perfume or 'aroma of sanctity'.

A famous story is told about the Italian Army Chief of Staff, General Luigi Cadorna, during World War I. He had a disastrous campaign while leading his ill-equipped forces against the might of Austria-Hungary and Germany. A series of setbacks culminated in the greatest fiasco of all – the collapse of his army in the face of an enemy attack in October 1917.

General Cadorna's soldiers were routed. They fled in disarray, resulting in over one-quarter of a million Italians surrendering to the enemy. The general was vilified and relieved of command. Driven to despair, and clearly depressed, he decided to take his life. The only thing that stopped him was a visit by a strange friar whose name he didn't know and whose existence he wasn't even aware of.

The story of what happened is now part of Padre Pio legend. While contemplating suicide, Cadorna smelled the perfume of roses and violets. Looking up, he saw before him a strange monk, with bleeding hands, who instructed him to be calm. This he did, heeding the advice of the mysterious intruder who then proceeded to vanish.

On speaking to his friends, General Cadorna was informed, 'That must have been Padre Pio.' Unaware of who the friar was, he acquired further information and paid a visit to San Giovanni in 1920. Once he saw Padre Pio, he immediately recognised him as the person who had come to him on the infamous night a few years before.

At the time, Padre Pio was gaining a reputation for his many supernatural gifts, among them his aroma of sanctity, or scent of roses, and his ability to bilocate, or to appear in two places at the same time. There would be numerous other examples of both in the decades to come – one of them concerning an Irishman, from County Cork, by the name of Sammy Revins, whose experiences relate to his terminally-ill wife, Mena.

'I never knew Padre Pio until sickness came along,' Sammy Revins explained. 'My wife Mena had cancer. Unfortunately, it was lung cancer. She had only a year or a year and a half to live.' On being told about Padre Pio by a friend whose daughter was sick, he turned to the future saint looking for help. 'From that day on we got involved with Padre Pio,' he said. 'I read an awful lot of the books on Padre Pio and we used to pray every night to him.

'Then, one Sunday morning, I got the smell of the roses. I thought it was beautiful. I got such a fright. I was lighting the fire, I went out for coal and the fragrance was out of this world. I looked around, there wasn't a sinner about. It was before first Mass. It was about April or May. I had no garden, I had no flowers. I went up to herself and I said it to her. She said, "Yes, I got it before."

'About a fortnight before she died we were in bed together and she woke me and said, "Do you smell that, Sammy?" I said, "I do, it's like cigarettes, like cigar smell." He came again, that was his presence again with us. You see, Padre Pio will come to people in this way to let them see that he is there, that he is with you.

'There was another night, coming near the end, and she tried to wake me. I used to be awake quite a lot at night. This night she couldn't wake me. When she did wake me I was in a ball of sweat. She said to me, "He was here." I said, "Who?" She said, "Padre Pio." She said, "I couldn't wake you, I am frozen but you are wringing with sweat." That was her privilege and he came to her. "It's either one thing or the other," she said, "either I'm not going to live very long more or I'm going to get better."

'I asked her what happened. She said, "He came into the room. His two big eyes were lighting up. He came over and I was getting afraid. I turned towards you but he said, 'Don't be afraid.' He put his hand on my shoulder and that was it. He went then."

'One thing she asked me to do was that I promise that I would go to San Giovanni for her. I said I would and I did. I will never forget what it was like when I got there. When I arrived at the church that evening, it was like as if someone pulled a screen across me and put everything out of my mind.

'The peace and the happiness and the contentment that was there was out of this world. I remember during the consecration

I said, "Will this be the end or will you still be with me?" The next minute there was a smell of violets, it was beautiful. Padre Pio is always there, he'll always help us and he always has.'

Teresa Deevy, one of Ireland's leading playwrights from the 1930s, paid a visit to San Giovanni Rotondo to witness Padre Pio.

A revealing story is told about the Irish playwright Teresa Deevy. While on a visit to Padre Pio in San Giovanni Rotondo, she had the misfortune of being picked up by an unscrupulous taxi driver. It was late at night. She was far from anywhere and she was alone. It seems the driver decided to make a financial killing at the expense of his passenger, who was not only a woman but completely deaf.

He began by attempting to charge her too much, but then proceeded to demand every lira out of her purse. Speaking in French – which she always did in Italy, believing it commanded more respect than English – she tore into the taxi driver and verbally beat him into submission. 'In the circumstances, you and I would have given in,' wrote Julia Monks in a diary piece in *The Irish Press*. 'Not so Miss Deevy.'

The diarist continued: 'Cocking her charcoal eyebrows at the brigand under the beam of his head-lamps, she let fly at him good and proper in her best French *argot* until he surrendered, bowed if unbloody, and drove her, as she requested, back to her hotel, where the statutory fare was worked out to the satisfaction of both parties. There's personality for you!'

Teresa Deevy was certainly a tough, independent woman, who travelled extensively and overcame serious adversity in her life. Born in Waterford in 1894, she began to go deaf in her late teens and early 20s. Her condition, caused by a disorder of the inner ear known as Meniere's disease, prompted her to travel to London where she learned lip-reading. Instead of inhibiting her interest in playwriting – after all, she couldn't hear dialogue – it may have enhanced her interest in words and how they are expressed.

Six of her plays were staged by the Abbey Theatre in Dublin in the 1930s, including *Temporal Powers*, *The King of Spain's Daughter* and *Katie Roche*. Soon, she was being compared to the female greats of the Irish stage. As fellow playwright James Cheasty put it: 'Teresa Deevy was, with the exception of Lady Gregory, the most memorable (of the Abbey women dramatists) and like Lady Gregory her name springs instantly to mind in any discussion on outstanding contributions by women writers to Anglo-Irish dramatic literature.'

More pertinently, from the perspective of this book, she was a staunch Catholic. Teresa was a daily Mass-goer and communicant. She was also a member of the Legion of Mary. Two of her sisters were nuns and her brother was a priest. Indeed, her religious convictions were such that she travelled, mostly alone, on pilgrimages to Lourdes, Assisi, Lisieux, Fatima, Rome and, of course, to see Padre Pio in San Giovanni Rotondo.

We know little or nothing about Deevy's visit to San Giovanni or her views of the future saint. Although we do know with certainty that the visit took place, she seemingly kept the details to herself. As her nephew Kyle Deevy once said, she was always 'guarded' about her life and revealed little. We can, however, speculate about what likely occurred.

She definitely attended the friar's Mass – everybody did – where she would have witnessed his intensity and shared in his general blessing. She could not have attended his confession as she had only a smattering of Italian. As a well-regarded Irish playwright – and an ardent Catholic – she would have been introduced to him probably in one of the friary corridors.

In Rome, on her way out and back to San Giovanni, no doubt she researched her forthcoming play *Supreme Dominion*, which was premiered in 1957. The play dealt with a fellow Waterford person and Franciscan friar, Luke Wadding, who lived in the late sixteenth and seventeenth centuries and spent much of his life in the Eternal City where, in 1625, he established the College of St. Isidore for the education of Irish priests. It wasn't one of her finest plays, described by *The Irish Press* as falling 'surprisingly short', and never catching fire and with 'many defects' according to the *Irish Independent*.

After a falling-out with the Abbey Theatre, Deevy turned to radio and had many of her plays broadcast on Radio Éireann. At that stage, she lived in Dublin, on Waterloo Road, with her sister Nell. They were very close, with an extraordinary ability to communicate.

'The ability of Tessa and Nell to converse was a mystery to me,' nephew Kyle remarked. 'After driving them from Athboy one night, I mentioned to Nell that I couldn't understand how Tessa knew what you were saying without light to see your lips. She assured me that there was no mystery as they had perfected their ability to talk under all conditions.'

Soon after the death of Nell in 1954, Deevy returned to Waterford, where she spent the rest of her life. She continued to write, devising scripts and ideas and producing reams of words, but with no notable success. Things were never the same. Although clearly one of Ireland's leading female playwrights, her name was soon largely forgotten. She died, just short of 69 years of age, in January 1963.

Sean Dunne, in *The Cork Examiner*, later wrote a wonderful description of her final years in Waterford, where she became a recognisable figure. 'In the Fifties,' he reflected, 'she was a thin woman on a bicycle, her grey hair tucked under one of an assortment of strange hats. She rode through the streets of Waterford and those who knew her tensed as she passed in case a car might hit her.

'She was completely deaf and somehow avoided being hit by the Morris Minors and Anglias that blared behind her. She heard nothing and just cycled on with the nonchalance of a girl cycling along a country road. Her clothes never seemed to match. She was seen wearing sandals or runners even in the middle of winter. Some people thought she'd once written plays. Others knew it, but it was a long time ago. Her name was Teresa Deevy.'

Fr. P. Hamilton Pollock, an Irish Dominican priest, met Padre Pio while serving as a chaplain in World War II. He later became prior of the Dominican community in Limerick.

It was late 1943 when a young Belfast-born chaplain by the name of Fr. P. Hamilton Pollock met Padre Pio. He was at the time attached to the Royal Air Force and had arrived at San Giovanni by a long and dangerous route. As fortune would have it, he had been ordained to the priesthood in September 1939, at a time when Czechoslovakia was already echoing to the sound of German Army goosesteps and the invasion of Poland had just begun. By the time of his arrival at San Giovanni, he was a chaplain in the RAF.

In 1941, Fr. Pollock had been summoned to Dublin by his Dominican superior, who requested that he join the British war effort. Chaplains were in short supply and he seemed like the perfect candidate. Agreeing to the suggestion, he found himself at the epicentre of the battles that raged throughout North Africa and Europe – accompanying the Allies through Algeria and Tunisia, across to Corsica and Sardinia, and on to the Italian mainland where advances were made step by step, house by house and street by street.

By a strange quirk of fate, Pollock ended up with Bomber Command near the town of Foggia, a short distance from San Giovanni and Padre Pio. Here the Allies assembled what may well have been the greatest armada of planes ever brought together in the history of flying. The attraction was simple – it was the only place suitable for heavy bombers to operate in a mountainous country. Foggia was also the town from which so many air and army personnel – from Britain and America, including Irish recruits – would travel the short distance to meet the future saint.

One day, a medical officer with one of the many assembled squadrons, an Irishman named Dr. Michael Hickey, asked Fr. Hamilton if he had ever heard of Padre Pio. The question triggered a vague recollection dating back to the time when he was a student. Was he not a stigmatic, he wondered, with wounds on his hands, feet and side? The very man, Dr. Hickey informed him, while also saying that he had met him only the day before. He was, he said, living in the Capuchin monastery in San Giovanni along with seven other friars.

The following week, Fr. Hamilton happened to be on a duty call in San Giovanni. His army jeep was co-piloted by a recruit named Tich. They drove up what appeared to be the only street in the village, at the end of which was a church with a monastery behind it. Having forgotten that this was the home base of Padre Pio, he suggested to Tich to wait as he called into the church to pray.

On entering, he noticed that one other person was inside, kneeling at the top of the church, deep in contemplation. 'One of the brown-robed priests was kneeling in front of the high altar,' he later wrote in *Wings on the Cross*, his autobiographical account of the war. 'His cowled head was inclined forward, his hands buried deep in the loose sleeves of his habit.' On seeing the priest, Pollock recalled the comment made by Dr. Hickey that Padre Pio was based in the village.

Quietly walking up the church, Fr. Hamilton approached the robed figure to ask where he might find Padre Pio. He tapped him on the shoulder. Deep in concentration, the bowed figure didn't respond. On tapping again, there was still no reply. A third time he tapped and this time the figure slowly looked up, his concentration broken but his eyes still blank. It was clear to Fr. Hamilton that he was in the presence of someone who was 'not of this earth' and 'very far removed from this world.' He instantly knew it was Padre Pio.

The Irish priest and the Capuchin walked out of the church together, where Fr. Hamilton explained that he was a chaplain with the Royal Air Force. Padre Pio held him in a tight embrace, leading him to believe that 'he, too, could be numbered amongst the large circle of friends of a saint.' For the first time he felt gratitude for World War II, that long and brutal conflict which had given him the chance to meet such a saintly, charismatic man.

Pollock introduced Tich to Padre Pio, explaining who he was and that he was non-Catholic. It made no difference – he, too, was embraced by the future saint. On their return journey to Foggia, Tich broke his uncustomary silence by asking, 'Father, is there something different about that man?' 'Why?' asked Fr. Pollock. 'Well, Father, when he embraced me I just wanted to lie there against him and never move again.' The priest understood fully what Tich meant by the remark.

Later on, Fr. Hamilton made sure that all Catholic military personnel under his care were afforded the opportunity to attend Padre Pio's Masses. This they did, witnessing the hands which although bandaged at other times were not bandaged during the service. 'His hands were beautifully chiselled as if made of white marble,' Pollock later recalled. 'The fingers were long and tapering, with half-moon nails. In the middle of each hand was a large raw open wound, sometimes covered with congealed blood.'

Following the Masses, troops would enter the sacristy and kiss the padre's hands. Soon, Protestants were coming to visit, too. Both Catholics and Protestants acquired medals which had been blessed by the friar. Catholics wore them on the collars of their flying jackets as symbols of their faith; Protestants wore them as lucky charms or simply out of respect for the remarkable person who had blessed them.

For the remainder of World War II, thousands of soldiers – representing multiple nationalities and religious creeds – made their way to be blessed by, or to hear Masses said by, Padre Pio. It was nothing short of bewildering how a worldwide conflagration brought so many to meet this strange mystic in a tiny village tucked away in the middle of nowhere, and how these pilgrims in turn brought word of this extraordinary stigmatic back to places like Boston and Chicago, Melbourne and Toronto, London and Dublin, and scores of other cities, towns and villages in between.

As Fr. Pollock put it in *Wings on the Cross*: 'Practically every soldier, friend or foe, from almost every nation in the world, who passed through Italy, was received into Padre Pio's spiritual family and through these soldiers Padre Pio's reputation as a saint was passed on to the rest of the world....All were received into his embrace and they just wanted to lie there against him and never move again.'

One of America's most famous songwriters, Irving Berlin, whose wife came from an Irish Catholic family, met Padre Pio in 1944.

During the winter months of 1943 – 1944, the Allied military advance through Italy was torturously slow. Violent blizzards, snowstorms, whiteouts and zero visibility confronted the armed forces as they fought their way up through the country all the way to Rome. Soldiers were tired, wistful and longing for an end to the war. Armed Forces Radio constantly played Bing Crosby's White Christmas to remind them of home.

Few of the troops realised that the song they were listening to was composed by a Jewish songwriter named Irving Berlin. Fewer still would have known that its sentimental undertones were inspired by the death on 25 December 1928 of his three-week-old son, whose grave he visited every Christmas Day. Above all, none of the soldiers could have guessed that within a matter of months the composer of the song would be performing before them in an action-packed musical review. Some would see him in Foggia, just down the road from Padre Pio.

By that stage of the war, Irving Berlin had become the most successful American songwriter in history. Although unable to read music, and only able to play the piano in one key, he was on his way to producing an astonishing array of songs including

Alexander's Ragtime Band, Puttin' On The Ritz, There's No Business Like Show Business, God Bless America, Always, and a stream of hit musicals including Top Hat and Annie Get Your Gun.

Berlin's background had been blighted by poverty. His father – an immigrant Jew – had fled persecution in Russia, where he had worked as an itinerant singer of liturgical chant music in synagogues. With seven children in tow, the family arrived in New York, where they struggled to survive. After the death of his father when Irving was just a young boy, he was forced to sell newspapers and sing on the streets to ensure that his family could eat. He later recalled how, at the time, he wore secondhand clothes and ate scraps.

It was probably no surprise that later in life, when he was in his mid-30s and had risen to great fame, he would meet and marry a woman from a similar background. Her name was Ellin Mackay, whose grandfather had been born in the slums of Dublin. Having emigrated to America with his sister and parents in 1840, her grandfather found himself in circumstances that could only be described as dire. He would die not long after his arrival in America, forcing his son – Ellin's father – to sell newspapers to support the family.

By the time the Jewish Irving Berlin and the Irish Catholic Ellin Mackay met in 1925, circumstances for both of them had changed dramatically. Ellin's father had tried his hand at gold and silver prospecting, initially failing miserably but eventually striking it rich. Along with his partners, he discovered what became known as the Comstock Lode, which was the largest silver ore lode in history. Their wealth was unimaginable for the time, even for today.

Irving Berlin had also made it rich following his initial success with Alexander's Ragtime Band in 1911. He had written hundreds of songs and many successful musicals for the stage. He was even part-owner of a Broadway theatre. As far as Ellin's father was concerned, however, there was one problem – he was Jewish and she was Irish Catholic. Undeterred, the couple married in 1926. Her father subsequently disowned her in his will.

World War II interrupted everything in the way that wars can only do. Putting his career on hold, Irving Berlin committed himself to the war effort and composed a musical to inspire and entertain the troops. After a hugely successful run in America, he was persuaded to bring the show on tour. This he did, travelling to Britain, North Africa and then to Italy, reaching Naples and then moving on to Foggia.

What we know today is that, despite being Jewish, Irving Berlin travelled in July 1944 from Foggia to San Giovanni Rotondo where he met Padre Pio. Something drew him to the place. Exactly what the 'something' might have been we don't know. He did have a cousin of his wife – Count Telfener – living in San Giovanni, and maybe that inspired the trip. Alternatively, he may have simply heard the rumours about a strange mystic living near Foggia and travelled to satisfy his curiosity.

Regarding the meeting between the two men, we know that they spoke for a time. Aware that his visitor was Jewish, the padre presented him with a thoughtful gift. The gift was meant, he said, not for the composer but for Ellin, who he knew was Catholic. It was a set of rosary beads, no doubt specially blessed by the future saint. That, I'm afraid, is the sum total of what we know about the famous songwriter's visit to Padre Pio in 1944 – the rest is lost to history.

Following his tour of Italy, Irving Berlin and his musical company moved to Egypt, where they performed at the Cairo Opera House, then to Iran, moving eventually across to the Pacific where their first performance was in New Guinea in December 1944. Soon, the war was over and he resumed his phenomenal career.

Arriving back in America exhausted, he set about composing again. He began with a musical based on the story of Annie Oakley, the American markswoman who was regarded as the finest sharpshooter in the Wild West. The show was an enormous success. Called Annie Get Your Gun, it contained numerous hit songs including There's No Business Like Show Business, My Defences Are Down and Anything You Can Do.

In the following years, he and Ellin lived in New York. They continued to do so until her death in 1988, aged 85, and his death the following year, aged 101. Inevitably, the tributes poured in, with the American composer Jerome Kern stating that 'Irving Berlin has no place in American music. He *is* American music,' and Ginger Rogers – who had danced with Fred Astaire to his tunes – stating that working with Irving Berlin had been 'like heaven.' She certainly used an appropriate allusion in the context of his visit to Padre Pio almost half a century earlier!

Irish-American William 'Bill' Carrigan, who was assigned to the Fifteenth Air Force during World War II, met Padre Pio many times in the war's final years.

It was during yet another local snowstorm that Irish-American Bill Carrigan first made his way up the steep, winding roads to San Giovanni Rotondo in the winter of 1943 – 1944. Packed into a U.S. Army truck along with other G.I.s, the group wound their way over the narrow, bumpy roads, battling the blizzards and snowdrifts that blocked their path.

They eventually arrived at a quiet, deserted San Giovanni, where visitors were scarce during the war years and, anyway, the bitter cold was keeping villagers indoors. Adding to the sense of emptiness and abandonment was Padre Pio's Mass which was already in progress and where the local faithful who had braved the bad weather were already assembled.

'We were taken into the sanctuary,' Bill Carrigan later wrote. 'We knelt on the cold marble floor on the side not ten feet from Padre, where we could observe his every movement. As he began the consecration he seemed to be in great pain, shifting his weight from side to side, hesitating to begin the words of consecration which he would start and repeat – biting them off with a clicking of his teeth as if in great pain.

'His cheek muscles twitched and tears were visible on his cheeks. He reached for the chalice and jerked back his hand because of the pain in the wound which was fully visible to me. After his communion he leaned over the altar for some time as if he was in communion with Jesus. Later I learned that at this time he presented his many spiritual children to Our Lord offering his own suffering for them.'

During that brief wartime visit, Bill Carrigan was smitten by Padre Pio, believing – even *knowing* – he was 'a witness to a saint in formation.' He was convinced, he wrote, that 'here was a priest who had attained a state of sanctity the like of which I had only read about, but never met before. In the sacristy after Mass we met for a few minutes. I received his blessing and was allowed to kiss the wound in his hands. I knew we had a destiny together. I sensed that I wanted to help make him known in America.'

In time, Bill Carrigan became one of the best-known voices espousing the cause of Padre Pio in America. In the meantime, back in the 1940s, there was work to be done and a war had to be won. As Director of the American Red Cross Field Office, which was attached to the Fifteenth Air Force in Foggia, he participated in the Allied advance up through Italy during the final years of World War II.

In his capacity with the Red Cross, Carrigan had access to transport, which proved essential in facilitating his multiple subsequent visits to San Giovanni. At Carrigan's instigation, these vehicles would also enable numerous G.I.s to meet Padre Pio and receive his blessings. He later wrote about these visits in a letter to Colonel John Laboon, the Allied Military Governor of the Foggia region. The letter was eventually published in many newspapers and distributed to American troops.

'After the Mass the men are permitted to go with him to the sacristy and kiss the wounds in his hands while he is unvesting,' Carrigan wrote. 'He wears fingerless gloves at all times except at Mass and the men seek the opportunity to kiss his hands while he is unvesting because he puts on the gloves as soon as he removes his alb. He is most patient and kind to all who come to him at this time, especially this is true for our soldiers who often get a word and a gentle pat on the cheek from him.

'At this time, I have often arranged for him to take our soldiers to a side room and give them his blessing, a word, perhaps, and bless their rosaries, or anything they might desire blessed. Many like him to bless their silver wings. His engaging smile and simple humility draw everyone to him.'

If it might appear that a mass invasion of American G.I.s from Foggia to San Giovanni was instigated by Bill Carrigan during the final years of the war, the truth is that's exactly what happened. Groups of soldiers would regularly beat a path to the friar. The Italian-Americans would engage with him in their language of origin; others, including Irish-Americans, would communicate through interpreters.

'When the soldiers board their trucks and begin the winding trip down the mountain, there is much silence and deep thought,' Carrigan wrote of their return trips to Foggia. 'When conversation starts, it is always about Padre Pio and what effect he had on them. Reactions vary greatly, but everyone reports an undefinable change in their being.

'One said he found Padre Pio looking at him as he entered the sacristy and in that moment he felt that Padre Pio could see right into his mind, and the sins of his whole life seemed to flash into his consciousness. Another man told me that he felt that his soul was given a profound shaking and his mind put to work at right thinking. Back in camp the soldiers think and talk about this wonderful priest and what he must be. All want to return again, most everyone has a buddy who wants to go, too.'

Bill Carrigan established a close bond with Padre Pio – staying at the monastery in a room near Padre Pio's and eating in the refectory with the friars – before eventually returning to America and spreading the word about this wonderful man in San Giovanni Rotondo. Back in America, he became highly successful as a businessman, remained devoted to his dear wife Ramona for 51 years, and practised his Catholic faith.

At the service following his death in November 2000, he was eulogised for his churchgoing habits. Even as a 93-year-old, it was said, he would attend Mass every morning no matter how bad the weather might be. After, or during, a heavy snowfall he would pull up in his car, ready for Mass. 'What the trip between his home and the church had been like was one of those things I expect you didn't really want to know,' it was remarked.

Up to his death, he also propagated the cause of Padre Pio, writing letters and newspaper columns, sponsoring videos and books, and organising Masses commemorating the future saint. It was said that, in his lifetime, he handed out more than 1,000,000 prayer cards featuring Padre Pio. He also attended the friar's beatification in 1999, but was called home before the canonisation in 2002.

'It is always a great honour for me to talk about Padre Pio,' Bill Carrigan once said. 'During the war it was amazing how he got things done, when there was not a single source of help around. In his 50 years in this ancient Capuchin monastery, always in prayer, bearing great suffering in body as well as in mind, he learned to value and use whatever God gave him.

'He established credibility – and this gave his people stability – even in all their rightful fears in the war years. He taught people how to bear their suffering and convert it to grace.' And how Bill knew all of this was simple – because 'I am a witness,' he concluded.

Leo Fanning, an Irish-American, had a strange encounter with Padre Pio towards the end of World War II. The event changed his life.

Leo Fanning was brought up in a traditional Irish-American family in Newburgh, Orange County, New York. Set on the banks of the Hudson River, the city, which was once the homeland of Native Americans and early planters, reeks of its historical past. Lots of Irish emigrants eventually settled there, bringing with them their fervent Catholicism and love of the country they had left behind.

Like many Irish-Americans in the early twentieth century, the Fanning family did well. One of his sisters went on to receive a Masters degree in education, which was an unusual achievement for its time; another sister studied at a business institute. Leo, who was born in 1922, had a hankering to become a priest but he kept the notion to himself. Anyhow, his ambitions were put on hold with the advent of World War II.

Having enlisted in the U.S. military, he was assigned to the 304th Bomb Wing of the Fifteenth Air Force. During the Allied advance up through Italy, the famous Fifteenth eventually set up base at Cerignola, about 40km south-east of Foggia. Leo was just celebrating his 21st birthday when he and his colleagues arrived at their new base.

Corporal Fanning, a practising Catholic, was soon informed about the extraordinary stigmatic living just over 80km away. He promised to meet him one day. Eventually, a window of opportunity opened and Leo travelled along with a friend to San Giovanni Rotondo, which, as so often the case at the time, was thronged with the faithful. The Mass having finished, they were waiting to have their confessions heard by Padre Pio.

Determined not to be denied an introduction to the friar, the two young men waited until the confessions were over. Suddenly, they had their chance. Approaching Padre Pio, Leo's friend, who spoke Italian, introduced himself. He then introduced his companion. 'This is Leo Fanning,' he said. 'Your name is not just Leone,' the padre immediately responded, using the Italian version of the name. 'Some day you will be *Padre* Leone.'

Quite understandably, Leo Fanning was taken aback. No mention had been made of his interest in entering the priesthood. There was no earthly way Padre Pio could have known what had been on his mind. No rational explanation could exist for what had just happened, other than that Padre Pio had read his soul.

Throughout the remainder of his time with the Fifteenth Air Force in Cerignola, Leo Fanning paid many further visits to San Giovanni, attending Padre Pio's Mass, meeting the stigmatic's fellow friars, and having many conversations with the future saint. Eventually, the time came for his return to America. He departed San Giovanni with great sadness in his heart.

Had Leo Fanning known of Padre Pio's previous record with predictions, he might not have been so surprised by what the padre had told him. As far back as 1919, he had predicted that a young boy would become a friar, which he did. On another occasion, he had foretold that a young woman would become a nun, which also came to pass. He had also remarked that only two out of six students in one seminary would become priests; regarding another seminary, he said that five out of 25 students would become friars – both predictions proved to be accurate.

Padre Pio was also accurate in his prediction concerning Leo Fanning. He eventually entered the Immaculate Conception Seminary in Mahwah, New Jersey, and was ordained to the priesthood in May 1954. He served as a priest for the remainder of his life. There was one strange footnote to his ordination, though. Just minutes before the ceremony, he was handed a telegram congratulating him on what was about to take place. It was signed 'Padre Pio.' How on earth, he wondered, could the man have known!

World-renowned author Graham Greene paid a visit to San Giovanni in 1949, with the intention of meeting Padre Pio.

By a peculiar twist of fate, the fortunes of author Graham Greene, Achill Island in County Mayo and the stigmatist Padre Pio crossed paths in the late 1940s. The common denominator was a woman named Catherine Walston, who had a long affair with Greene, often conducted at her rented cottage on the island, and who accompanied him on his famous visit to San Giovanni to meet the future saint.

Walston was an intriguing woman – wife of the British life peer and millionaire, Henry Walston, better known in political circles as Baron Walston. Although married, she conducted an affair with Greene that scandalised British society and lasted from 1946 to the mid-1960s. Some of their most memorable times were spent together at their modest, somewhat primitive, island retreat.

It was on Achill that Greene composed parts of some of his novels, notably *The Heart of the Matter*, adding to his fine collection of works including *Brighton Rock*, *Our Man in Havana* and *The Honorary Consul*. The location offered peace and tranquillity, no doubt of great value to a writer interested in spiritual matters and who had earlier in life converted to Catholicism. Perhaps it was this fascination with his faith that inspired him to visit San Giovanni in 1949.

Like all great Greene novels, the visit had many twists and turns. For a start, although he was married and a convert to Catholicism since 1926, he was also known for his extramarital affairs. The greatest of his illicit romances was with his beloved Catherine. It seems ironic that these two parties – Graham and Catherine – would set out together to visit a man known for his capacity to see into the dark recesses of people's souls.

Having travelled to Rome, where Greene had an audience with Pope Pius XII, the couple then moved on to San Giovanni. What happened there can be gleaned from a letter he sent to author Kenneth L. Woodward from Antibes in 1990, not long before he died; and from an interview he did with his biographer Norman Sherry for his trilogy of biographies, *The Life of Graham Greene*.

Greene explained how it was arranged for him to meet Padre Pio in the monastery, but he got cold feet and backed out. The reason he gave was that neither he nor Catherine wanted their lives changed. To interpret the remark, we might suppose that Greene anticipated that the friar would read his soul and offer guidance about the steps they should take. It was an issue he didn't want to face.

Both Greene and Catherine, however, did attend Padre Pio's early Mass, securing a place very close to the altar. He could clearly see the padre's ungloved hands, with dried blood encasing the stigmata, the blood at one moment becoming wet and the next moment drying. Although he regularly attempted to pull his sleeves over the stigmatised hands, they kept coming back up and revealing the wounds once more. Unlike his hands, which were exposed, Padre Pio's feet were swathed in bandages, to stop the wounds from bleeding.

Greene was surprised by how quickly the Mass passed by. He had been told it would last a long time but, at its finish, he felt it had lasted less than an hour. To the contrary, he discovered when he emerged from the chapel that it had lasted two hours. He was baffled by how the time had slid by so quickly. Time, as so many have said about Padre Pio, took on a different dimension in his presence.

Following his 1949 visit to San Giovanni, Graham Greene returned to a life much as it had been before. The affair with Catherine Walston continued for many years. His ambiguous and paradoxical relationship with Catholicism remained unresolved. Even on his deathbed in Switzerland, as he received communion, he still had a mistress in Antibes, France.

The one thing, however, that never faltered was his belief in Padre Pio. As he grew old, many decades after his return from San Giovanni, he still recalled the event in vivid detail. He also spoke disparagingly about a remark made to him by a monsignor in Rome, around the time of the visit, that Padre Pio was 'a pious old fraud.' And he kept a photo of the future saint in his wallet right up to the day of his death in April 1991. If nothing else, that was a mark of pure faith.

One of Ireland's most respected authors, Seán Ó Faoláin, also visited Padre Pio.

It seems ironic that the renowned author Graham Greene was the person who encouraged Seán Ó Faoláin to go to Italy. He first suggested a visit to Ó Faoláin in 1947, mentioning that he knew publishers who would pay handsome expenses in lieu of a travel book on the country. Greene, who knew Italy well, no doubt informed Ó Faoláin of the many places he might visit, most of which the Irish author travelled to over the coming years.

The irony was compounded by the fact that, just like Greene, Ó Faoláin was having an adulterous affair at the time. His lover, Honor Tracy, accompanied him on at least one of his Italian visits and was referred to in a subsequent book, *Summer in Italy*, as a man named Ginger. Even though Ó Faoláin loved the lighter brand of Catholicism in Italy, where passions ran high and affairs were commonplace, he was still consumed by Catholic guilt over his relationship with his beloved Honor.

When Ó Faoláin paid his first visit to Italy, he was already a well-established Irish writer. Born in Cork and a graduate of University College Dublin and Harvard University, he had served time with the IRA from 1918 – 1921 and had worked as their publicity director. He had also taught in Ireland, lectured in the USA, written wonderful short stories including *A Born Genius*, novels such as *A Nest of Simple Folk* and *Bird Alone*, and comprehensive biographies of Éamon de Valera and Daniel O'Connell.

We do not know if Honor Tracy accompanied Ó Faoláin on his post-war visit to San Giovanni Rotondo. What we do know, however, is that the author made his way via Foggia, where he attended the opera *Rigoletto*, and the next morning boarded the local bus for its slow journey up through the grim, rock-strewn landscape, all the way to San Giovanni. The bus was filled with pilgrims who were intent on visiting, and hopefully meeting, the stigmatic friar.

Ó Faoláin's descriptions of his arrival at the village are visually wonderful. They are variously contained in his book *South to Sicily*, which was published in America under the title *An Autumn in Italy*, and in articles in *The Irish Digest* and *Commonweal* magazine. He described the dusty piazza, with its scattering of trees, political slogans on the walls, clothes hanging out to dry, and a cinema poster showing the actor Robert Taylor kissing a blonde in semi-undress. Just a short distance up the hill one could see the weather-worn chapel, cloister walls and pilgrims hanging about 'as patiently as dray horses.'

As Ó Faoláin waited by the chapel, he was suddenly aware of a bearded friar, 'brown robed, brown eyed, stern looking,' making his way through the unruly mob. Then, an extraordinary thing happened. Directly in front of the friar, and blocking his way, was a sallow, keen-eyed youth. Without pausing, Padre Pio cried out in Italian, 'Begone, Satan!' The youth, as Ó Faoláin put it, wavered, paled and slunk back into the mob.

Later that day, Ó Faoláin met the young man and asked him for an explanation of the event. He said that he was a clerk from Milan, an agnostic, a non-believer, who had undergone a major operation the previous year and had only come to San Giovanni to make his mother happy. Interested in seeing what the friar was like, he was standing there, looking, saying nothing as Padre Pio approached. 'I can tell you he frightened me when he said, "Begone, Satan!"' he remarked. 'I do not know how he knew that I am an agnostic.'

This extraordinary insight to the attributes of Padre Pio certainly left its mark on Ó Faoláin. Not only did the strange happening embed itself on his mind, but so too did the power and magnetism of the man who was at the centre of it. Although Ó Faoláin described the friar as an 'ordinary, healthy, grizzled, stoutish, middle-aged, tired-looking man,' he was likewise struck by the blaze and warmth of Padre Pio's personality. He was, in short, an unforgettable man, Ó Faoláin concluded.

During his visit, Ó Faoláin was introduced to the stigmatist. 'When I spoke to him he became jovial, almost hearty, laughed with pleasure when he heard that I was Irish and laid his two hands warmly and affectionately on my head in benediction,' Ó Faoláin wrote in his book *South to Sicily*. 'Thousands have spoken to him, found him, as I did, kindly and jovial, amiable and kind, and because his humanity is so evident his saintliness is all the more impressive.'

Like many who came to visit, Ó Faoláin was specially moved by Padre Pio's confessions. Although he could not attend them himself, without proficiency in Italian or Latin, he sat there watching the strange event. Surrounded by crowds of people, penitents knelt before the friar, recounting their sins and expressing their remorse. The padre listened to each person intently, taking such a long time that even Ó Faoláin became exhausted from just watching.

So great was the love of God shown by Pio that one could understand how he bore the stigmata, Ó Faoláin mused. So powerful was his link to the Divine that he imprinted on himself the marks of Christ's great tragedy. The thought also crossed the Irishman's mind that here was a man who had his wounds scarred into him by rays of light similar to those that penetrated St. Francis, while so many of his worshippers reached out their hands to him hoping to intercept those very rays which had poured from the body of God.

After staying that night in San Giovanni, Ó Faoláin set out the following morning to continue his travels throughout Italy. He ended up loving the country. All his encounters warmed his heart. He even reignited the Catholicism he once had but had left behind. Although formally excommunicated since Ireland's Civil War, he made a vigorous confession in St. Peter's and concluded that he once again 'felt emancipated as man and as artist.'

How much Padre Pio had to do with all this life renewal, no one knows. What we do know, however, is that – just as with Graham Greene – Ó Faoláin's visit to the friar would never be forgotten. The stigmatic, he concluded, was indeed 'a truly saintly man.' A modest, amiable, magnetic Italian, it wasn't difficult to imagine him being considered a saint, he believed. It might take half a century for the formal canonisation to happen, but even back then Ó Faoláin's instincts weren't far off the mark!

Author and former wartime spy, John McCaffery, who lived in County Donegal, became a personal friend of Padre Pio from the end of World War II up to the friar's death in 1968.

John McCaffery would often sit in his study in County Donegal and admire a painting hanging over the fireplace. It was a fine work of art, an original portrait by the artist Antonio Ciccone, who had studied his craft in the finest studios in Florence and at the city's art academy. He would later become one of the world's foremost portrait painters, working especially in charcoal and acrylic.

There was an interesting connection between the painting – a large, life-like portrait of Padre Pio – its owner and the artist who created it. The artist Antonio Ciccone had been born in San Giovanni in 1939 and it was from there, under the guidance of Padre Pio, that he had been sent off on his studies in 1954, at the age of 14. His works would later hang in museums and private collections worldwide.

During the same era – the 1950s – John McCaffery was becoming not just acquainted with Padre Pio but establishing himself as one of his dearest friends. The relationship would continue for decades. In the circumstances, it seems appropriate that McCaffery would end up with a Ciccone portrait of the friar at his Donegal home, which he would frequently look at and smile.

Years before that, McCaffery had led an extraordinary life. A former student priest, who had been born in Scotland and studied in Rome, he had gone on to become the head of Britain's

Special Operations Executive in Europe during World War II. Based in Bern, in neutral Switzerland, he recruited resistance fighters in occupied countries, organised sabotage campaigns, and collected intelligence in a country that became the hub of Europe's covert operations during the war.

While in Bern, John McCaffery first became acquainted with Padre Pio through the head of the Italian operations in the city. Although on opposing sides, Don Rizzi and McCaffery knew each other well. It was Rizzi who first mentioned the remarkable friar to McCaffery; he also gave him a book on the future saint. McCaffery wasn't particularly interested.

Following the war, another of McCaffery's contacts – former *Times* journalist, historian and editor of *The Tablet*, Douglas Woodruff – discussed the stigmatic with McCaffery. Although astonished that a writer of such talent and intellect, who was being compared favourably to G.K. Chesterton and Hilaire Belloc, was interested in the stigmatic, it still took some time before McCaffery visited San Giovanni.

On his first visit to the monastery, undertaken appropriately on St. Patrick's Day, McCaffery was blown away by the man he encountered. Not only did he attend Padre Pio's Mass, but he also secured an introduction. He was overcome by the sense of holiness, kindness and sheer sincerity of the friar, to such an extent that he would remain forever under his spell. From that day until Padre Pio's death, he would become one of the most frequent overseas visitors to the monastery at San Giovanni Rotondo.

From the beginning, the two men became close friends. They would talk together, share jokes and at times even sit in the same stall together in the choir loft of the church. McCaffery was soon given the privilege of entering the monastery on his own and without special permission. He was also afforded the honour of serving at Padre Pio's Masses on seven occasions.

Soon, he was witnessing great miracles associated with this extraordinary mystic. In one case, a blind man's sight was restored; in another, a man was cured of cancer; in further cases, Padre Pio had read people's souls; in even more cases, his perfume or 'odour of sanctity' had been detected by people either in San Giovanni or a long distance away.

He was also informed of strange happenings involving Padre Pio's ability to bilocate. Among them was a remarkable story recounted first-hand by a friar. It seems that, one evening, Pio attended a concert in the monastery and apparently enjoyed the show. During the interval, however, he sat rigid with concentration, as if in a trance.

The following day, his fellow friar went to visit a house in the village where a person was known to be unwell. Not only was the patient restored to good health but the rest of the family was overjoyed. It quickly became clear why that was so. They explained that Padre Pio had visited them the previous evening, something which his fellow friar knew he could not have done as he had never left the monastery. When he asked what time Pio had visited, he discovered it was the same time as the concert interval. He wasn't in the least bit surprised.

A further story was related to John McCaffery about the experience of an American bomber pilot during World War II. Acting as squadron leader on a mission to bomb a target close to Foggia, he was confronted in the sky by the figure of a monk urging him to turn back. This he did, with inevitable consequences for his flying career. Having later been informed by an Italian that what happened may not have been so extraordinary after all, as a mystical friar lived in the region, he vowed to return one day. Following the war, the moment he saw Padre Pio in San Giovanni, he knew it was the same monk he had encountered on his mission.

Even McCaffery had his own strange experience to report, this time involving a miraculous cure. Since his wartime exploits, he had suffered from serious heart trouble, involving palpitations, head pain and a partial stroke. During a Mass in San Giovanni, he concentrated hard and mentally begged Padre Pio to help him avoid another stroke, which he feared to be imminent.

After the Mass, Padre Pio spontaneously held McCaffery's head in his hands and pressed it against the wound in his side. He did the same again on two further occasions. At other times, he spontaneously placed his stigmatised right hand against McCaffery's heart. No heart trouble was ever experienced again by McCaffery.

Following Padre Pio's death, in 1968, John McCaffery never set foot again in San Giovanni and never felt any urge to visit the friar's tomb. Instead, he treasured the wonderful memories he had of his former Capuchin friend and counted himself lucky to have known a man so holy, so warm-hearted, and so close to God. He also knew that the friar was still with him if not in body then certainly in spirit.

Eventually, John McCaffery wrote a wonderful book, *The Friar of San Giovanni: Tales of Padre Pio*, which was published in 1978. He also continued to live in County Donegal, where he and his wife farmed the land. And there they remained, surrounded by mementoes of Padre Pio – photos of McCaffery next to the friar, personally-blessed holy medals, part of a bloodstained bandage, some hair clippings, holy pictures with prayers handwritten by Padre Pio on them, not to mention a wonderful painting by Antonio Ciccone hanging in the study to remind him of the finest friend he ever had.

Barbara Ward, Assistant Editor of the *Dublin Review*, rescued Padre Pio's ailing ambition to build his ambitious hospital, Casa Sollievo della Sofferenza, at San Giovanni Rotondo, becoming a lifelong friend of the padre as a result.

In 1836, a Catholic quarterly publication called the *Dublin Review* was established to propagate Catholic doctrine and philosophy. One of its co-founders was Daniel O'Connell, the Kerry-born political figurehead who campaigned for greater rights for Irish Catholics – Catholic emancipation – and the repeal of the Act of Union binding Ireland to Great Britain.

The publication was an impressive one, highbrow and influential, staying in business until 1969 and reaching a significant audience not only in Ireland but also in Great Britain and elsewhere. It covered topics such as Society and the Church, The True View of the Protestant Reformation, Islamic Mysticism, Prayer in the Benedictine Rule, not to mention a critique of Dublin 'intellectual' writers and how far they were removed from true Irish feeling – all examined from a Catholic point of view.

What is little known about the review, however, is that one of its most prominent contributors, who was also its Assistant Editor, became not only close to Padre Pio but was instrumental in securing a huge injection of finance for the friar's dream hospital in San Giovanni Rotondo. Some 250 million lira ended up being provided to the project as a result of the *Dublin Review* contributor's efforts.

The person in question was no ordinary individual but an extraordinary woman named Barbara Ward. She was born in 1914, in England, to a Quaker father and a Roman Catholic mother. Brought up as a Catholic, she studied at the Sorbonne and Oxford before undertaking postgraduate work in mainland Europe where she witnessed the rise of Hitler.

Ward eventually returned to Britain where she wrote for *The Economist*, published numerous books, received an honorary doctorate from Harvard University, moved part-time to America where she worked as a professor at Columbia University, advised Presidents John F. Kennedy and Lyndon B. Johnson, and of course wrote for, and became Assistant Editor of, the *Dublin Review*.

Her link to Padre Pio was a remarkable one. In 1948, she travelled to Italy to write an article for *The Economist* about the country's post-war reconstruction. While there, she met with a friend of hers, the Marquess Patrizi, who also happened to be a friend of author Graham Greene. Together with the Marquess, she travelled to San Giovanni where she spoke to many of those involved in the planning and building of the hospital.

The big issue, she discovered, was a shortage of money. A priest informed her that with Padre Pio unwilling to take out bank loans, the only money available was from 'whoever passes by.' After Padre Pio provided the first coin to the hospital fund, subscriptions had come in but they were far from sufficient to complete the project. The friars needed a miracle. As it happened, the timing of the meeting was propitious – Barbara Ward needed a miracle, too.

Back in Britain, Barbara had a fiancé, Robert Jackson, who worked as a deputy director of the United Nations Relief and Rehabilitation Administration, which was vested with the task of helping rebuild Europe after World War II. With a Scottish father and Irish mother, he happened to be a member of the Anglican Church, creating difficulties for his pending marriage.

Ward, who was a devout Catholic, wanted Robert to convert to Catholicism. When she met Padre Pio, she asked if he could help bring a conversion about. He told her that if God willed it, it would happen. When she asked how long that might take, he replied that if God willed it, it would happen at that very moment.

She later learned that at the hour and day she presented her request to Padre Pio, Robert Jackson entered a Jesuit church in London and asked to convert to Catholicism. The couple married at St. Felix Church, Felixstowe, East Suffolk, in November 1950.

At the instigation of Barbara Ward, Robert Jackson sprang into action. Persuaded that a hospital would be of immense value to the war-torn region around Foggia, he secured from his organisation the sum of 400 million lira. It was a staggering amount of money at the time. Unfortunately, channelled through the Italian government, only 250 million lira of the total reached the project at San Giovanni, which infuriated Padre Pio for the remainder of his days.

The funding, although depleted, proved invaluable and the project steamed ahead. When Barbara and Robert visited San Giovanni in the autumn of 1950, they were both impressed by the manner in which the funds had been used. Barbara was even more taken by the visage of Mary in the altar's stained-glass window – it resembled her own. She was told that that was the intention – she was, after all, the godmother of the project!

Barbara Ward's connection with Padre Pio didn't end there. She later developed cancer but it went into remission, largely she believed because of help from Padre Pio. Unfortunately, in 1968 – during the same year as Padre Pio's death – the cancer reappeared, resulting in her being subjected to an operation and cobalt therapy to kill tumour tissue. Once again, she survived and continued to live a productive life, although at a slower pace.

In 1976, Barbara Ward was made a life peer, becoming Baroness Jackson of Lodsworth. She continued to write books, publishing another successful title in 1979 – *Progress for a Small Planet* – which dealt with global pollution, the exhaustion of limited resources and the growing divergence between the rich and the poor.

In that same decade – the 1970s – her marriage to Robert Jackson fell apart, but ever the devout Catholic she sought a separation as she didn't wish to divorce. Then, in May 1981, aged just 67, she died, leaving behind a rich legacy of work as a fine development economist and also as the woman who, by a strange combination of events, became one of the most important contributors to realising Padre Pio's dream of building a state-of-the-art hospital in San Giovanni Rotondo – a hospital which continues to serve his memory to this day.

Irish journalist Alan Bestic investigated one of Padre Pio's most famous miracles – the story of Giovanni Savino who, in 1949, inexplicably regained his sight following a traumatic accident. The interview was conducted in San Giovanni Rotondo, where the two men also met the future saint.

On a visit to San Giovanni in the 1960s, Dublin journalist Alan Bestic had the rare good fortune to interview a man whose miraculous recovery from sight loss following a major explosion had made headlines around the world. Bestic, who had previously written for *The Irish Times*, was working as a freelance journalist with the English tabloid press when he secured his remarkable interview. His later assignments included a dangerous trip to cover the Irish Army's mission to the Congo in the early 1960s, which he undertook for *The People on Sunday*.

His Congolese adventure made headlines when, on a return trip to the region, he was reported missing and feared to be taken hostage or dead. The Congolese could only confirm that an 'Alan Bestic, Irish passport number 64907,' had disappeared off their radar, and only God knew where he was. He turned up safely, however, and went on to produce some brilliant journalism throughout his career. His work included an interview with the stigmatic Therese Neumann of Bavaria, reports on the shrines of Fatima and Knock, and five books based on his worldwide travels. His output was both impressive and prolific.

Equally impressive was his interview with Giovanni Savino, who lived in San Giovanni and had earned his living as a labourer. In February 1949, he was employed on a project at the friary. The friars were building a new extension to their property, a task which required rock in the garden to be blasted with explosives. Given the time of year, when construction work was scarce, Savino was no doubt appreciative of the money.

Each morning, Savino, who was a believer in Padre Pio and known to the future saint, would attend the friar's Mass. He would then go to the sacristy for a blessing. 'I would ask Padre Pio for his blessing and kiss his hand,' he recalled. Later, he would join with his colleagues and set about his work.

One day, Padre Pio said something very mysterious while in the sacristy. 'He embraced me and said: "Courage.......don't worry,"' Savino remembered. 'I asked him what he meant, but he did not answer.' Over the next two days, the padre repeated his remarks, without elaborating. Savino was worried that something bad was about to happen.

On 15 February, he was sufficiently concerned to explain to his fellow workers what Padre Pio had said and to ask that they should not work that day. They ignored his plea. Instead, they set about the task of blasting boulders in the garden. Savino joined them, unaware of the tragedy that was about to occur.

That afternoon, an explosive charge was placed under a boulder, the fuse set alight and the explosion awaited. Nothing happened. After delaying for a while, Savino approached the charge to fix it in the hope it would work again. Suddenly, the dynamite 'exploded in my face,' he remarked.

His face was lacerated, his right eye destroyed, his left eye possibly destroyed, too. Whatever chance there was of saving his left eye, there was no hope for the one on the right. He was operated on in the hospital in nearby Foggia and his face was swathed in bandages. He was unconscious for three days. Everyone agreed that the prospects were grim.

'They did what they could for me in hospital, but I was in pretty bad shape,' Savino told Bestic. 'A few days later my doctor visited Padre Pio, who asked how I was. He told the padre: "I don't think he will live." And Padre Pio said: "I shall pray that he will receive the Grace."'

'That night I was lying in hospital, my eyes bandaged, my rosary in my hand. I felt two taps on my right eye and I cried out: "Who's that?" Then I smelled violets, and I knew. It was the perfume that sometimes surrounds Padre Pio.....what we call the odour of sanctity. I heard a voice, too, which left me in no doubt. It said: "We have received the Grace. We must pray always to God and Santa Lucia." It was the voice of Padre Pio.'

The following morning, Savino was examined by his doctor, who wanted to check if there was any hope of recovering the sight in his damaged left eye. On removing the bandages, Savino exclaimed, 'Doctor, I can see your hand!' Even though the right eye was like mashed jelly, an examination revealed that it was the right eye he was seeing through, and he could see through it perfectly. The doctor said: '"It's impossible,"' Savino recalled. 'But I could see, and when I convinced him, he said: "It's a miracle."

'My face was still badly scarred, of course. They wanted to use plastic surgery on me, but I would not let them. And, sure enough, my wounds healed and left no scar. But that is not all. When I came out of hospital, I went to Padre Pio to wish him a happy Easter and thank him for what he had done. He said: "We must thank God. I prayed for you hard because you caused me such suffering." I knew then it was true what they say..... that he suffers for us.'

Following their conversation, Bestic and Savino walked to the church, where Padre Pio was about to say Benediction. Although Bestic was a non-Catholic, he knelt beside Savino through the service and blessing. Afterwards, they made their way to the sacristy, where Padre Pio was disrobing.

'When he had finished, he walked through the aisle of waiting, kneeling people,' Bestic remarked. 'Giovanni stretched out for his hand and his eyes were glazed with emotion. The Capuchin seemed embarrassed by his reception and I had the feeling that he was trying to joke his way through what was obviously an ordeal for a shy and humble man. "Oho!" he said, as he came to Giovanni. But he smiled a gentle smile and held out his hand to be kissed.'

Later, Alan Bestic reflected on the authenticity of Giovanni Savino's miracle. There was no doubt, he said, that he was an honest man. He was satisfied that Savino had been gravely injured and had made a swift and amazing recovery. He was also convinced of Savino's certainty that, using his gift of bilocation, Padre Pio had stood by his bed that night in the hospital in nearby Foggia. Nor was there any doubt in Bestic's mind that Savino had smelled the perfume of violets.

'It was a strange encounter,' Bestic concluded. 'But then the unusual happens frequently at San Giovanni Rotondo.'

THE MIDDLE YEARS

1950 – 1959

There was a whiff of change in the air in 1950s Ireland. Although rightly regarded as 'the lost decade', the country was slowly finding its feet. Aer Lingus opened new routes to Europe, including Rome. The Cork Film Festival was launched, Ronnie Delany won gold at the Olympics, new economic plans were laid, and people like Brendan Behan and Samuel Beckett achieved fame abroad.

The Irish who had money – business people and professionals – headed off to see Padre Pio. Journalists were sent to compile reports. The Church – at the peak of its powers – had priests and prelates scuttling between Dublin and Rome, with some visiting San Giovanni. Add in the intensely curious and devout, and you have an accurate profile of those who found their way to Padre Pio in the 1950s.

The following is the story of a pope who loved Ireland and Padre Pio. The story begins in 1951, when some unexpected visitors arrived at the Cistercian abbey in Roscrea.

Monday, 10 September 1951 was an overcast, showery day, not quite the sort of weather one would expect for that time of the year. It was just coming up to noon. The Cistercian monks of St. Joseph Abbey, Roscrea, were going about their normal business when a Ford Anglia pulled up at their door. A man wearing the unmistakable purple sash of a monsignor emerged, with a favour to ask.

He explained that he had in the car a Monsignor Montini and they would like to have lunch and a tour of the abbey. 'Is that Monsignor Montini, the Pro-Secretary of State to the pope?' he was asked by the incredulous monk who stood before him. 'The very man,' the monsignor replied. It later turned out that the person asking the favour was Monsignor Benelli, Vatican charge d'affaires to Ireland, while another man sitting in the car was Monsignor McGeogh, a staff member of the Vatican Secretariat of State.

The visiting dignitary, Monsignor Giovanni Battista Montini, to give him his full name, had just landed at Shannon Airport having returned from a special mission to America on behalf of Pope Pius XII. He was on his way to Dublin where he planned to catch a flight to Rome. At the time, the visit was important as far as the monks at Roscrea were concerned. Twelve years later, the visit took on a greater significance when the monsignor became Pope Paul VI.

Those who met Montini during his brief stopover in 1951 later recalled him as 'a man of magnetic personality.' They weren't far off the mark, reflecting a widely-held, popular view. One of the monsignors who accompanied him at Roscrea wasn't wide of the mark either when he commented after Montini had briefly left the room they were in, 'That man will be pope someday.' Both remarks proved to be prescient when three years later he became Archbishop of Milan, and four years after that he was elevated to the College of Cardinals. But he still had one more step to go.

No one knew better than Padre Pio that Montini would one day become pope. They had met each other at the opening of the hospital, Casa Sollievo della Sofferenza, in San Giovanni, in May 1956. At the time, Montini was Archbishop of Milan. Later, Padre Pio requested that a message be relayed to the archbishop warning him that he would eventually become pope and to be prepared. When Montini received the message, he laughed and remarked how 'saints' came up with the strangest of ideas.

Padre Pio was having a lot of 'strange ideas' about future popes, not only regarding Montini but every other pope who was elected during his lifetime. It has been said that he correctly predicted the outcome of every papal election. We are uncertain whether that is true. What we do know, however, is that after the death of Pope John XXIII in 1963, Padre Pio's fellow friars pressed him – one might even say 'hounded' him – in an effort to find out who the next pope might be. Irritated and exasperated by the constant questioning, he finally told them to please be quiet – it was going to be Montini.

Just two years before his elevation to the papacy, Montini paid another visit to Ireland, staying at the Apostolic Nunciature in Dublin and visiting President Éamon de Valera. He had other

Irish connections, too – being taught to speak English by an Irish Christian Brother, establishing a close friendship with President of Ireland Seán T. O'Kelly, and later, as pope, delivering the homily at the canonisation Mass for St. Oliver Plunkett in Rome.

He was well aware of the Troubles in Ireland, once describing them as a 'festering sore.' Indeed, his family were also familiar with the Irish struggle for self-government, with his brother Ludovico Montini once chairing a Rome University meeting protesting the execution of Kevin Barry. Ludovico, who was a student at the time, subsequently became a lawyer and a member of the Italian parliament.

In late June 1963, 80 cardinals entered conclave at the Vatican Palace in Rome to elect the successor to Pope John XXIII. Voting began on a Thursday without any result. On the Friday morning, at 11.20 a.m. Irish time, white smoke trickled and then flowed steadily from the chimney on top of the Sistine Chapel. Shortly after midday, the 10,000 people in St. Peter's Square were informed that their new pontiff was Cardinal Giovanni Battista Montini, Archbishop of Milan. From then on, he would be referred to as Pope Paul VI.

Padre Pio, who had turned 76 the previous month, was in poor health at the time. Worn down by the stigmata and age, he was weak, arthritic, with swollen feet, shortness of breath and chest pains caused by bronchitis and asthma. He was also worn out by the investigations that had continued right into his 70s, resulting in many restrictions still being imposed on his activities.

Pope Paul VI would soon change all that. He accused one cardinal of treating Padre Pio 'like a criminal.' Just weeks after taking office, he instructed that the stigmatic should be liberated from all restrictions to 'make the work of Padre Pio easy so that he can fulfil his apostolate.' Instantly, Pio was no longer required to say Mass at abnormal times of the day; was allowed to meet visitors in the sacristy; and was told he could talk to anyone he wished following confession. The changes may have come late, but they did come, and they arrived thanks to the new pontiff.

We should not be surprised to learn that Padre Pio was profoundly grateful for the kindness of Pope Paul VI. It instilled in him a great sense of loyalty to his benefactor. That loyalty was so potent and intense that, on 12 September 1968, he wrote to the Holy Father pledging his fidelity and support.

The contents of the letter are touching to read. 'I offer Your Holiness my daily prayers and sufferings,' he wrote, 'the insignificant but sincere offering of the least of your sons, asking the Lord to comfort you with His grace to continue along the direct yet often burdensome way – in defence of those eternal truths which can never change with the times.'

After offering his support for the pope's encyclical, Humanae Vitae, he concluded: 'Prostrate at Your feet, I beg you to bless me, my Brothers in religion, my spiritual sons, the "Praying Groups", all the sick – that we may faithfully fulfil the good works done in the Name of Jesus and under your protection. Your Holiness' most humble servant, Padre Pio, Capuchin.'

Eleven days later, Padre Pio was dead.

One of the organisers of The Great Escape in World War II not only ended up living in Donegal but made a visit to Padre Pio in the early 1950s.

The first POWs entered the tunnel at 10.30 p.m. on 24 March 1944. It stretched from hut number 104 to the forest outside. Inside the perimeter fence was the prison compound Stalag Luft III in German-occupied Poland; outside was freedom and a 1,000-mile journey home.

Seventy-six Allied airmen made it through the tunnel that night. For more than a year they had moved earth, sunk shafts, forged passports, made imitation German guns, uniforms and ordinary civilian clothes, and devised their routes back to England. This was to be their moment of glory.

Of the 76 who escaped, 73 were recaptured, most of them within days. Fifty of the 73 were executed by the Gestapo on the orders of Adolf Hitler and Hermann Göring. The number 50 was chosen by Himmler, head of the SS. After being shot, the bodies of the airmen were cremated and returned to Stalag Luft III as an example to those left behind.

One of the prisoners back in the camp was a 33-year-old bomber pilot named Nicolas Tindal. A key organiser of what would eventually be immortalised in the movie *The Great Escape*, he had handed over his place on the escape list to a

Polish airman whose wife was due to give birth in England. Unfortunately, that pilot never made it to see his baby being born; he was among those executed.

NicolasTindal was born in 1911, in Dublin, where he studied Botany at Trinity College. After joining the RAF, he ended up as commander of a bomber squadron during World War II. Relatively early in the war, in December 1940, he was shot down over France and ended up as a prisoner of war.

Far from being a model prisoner, as far as the Germans were concerned, Tindal made many attempts to escape, including one eight-day venture lasting until he was arrested near Hamburg in a German uniform. He was also, of course, a central figure in organising the escape from Stalag Luft III.

Following the war, Tindal worked his way back to Ireland and settled down in County Donegal. Running his own farm, he effectively disappeared from public view. Despite all the excitement over the 1963 blockbuster movie *The Great Escape*, starring Steve McQueen, little was heard of this bomber pilot and his role in one of the most famous ventures in the history of World War II.

By chance, the author of this book noticed a reference to Tindal's name in John McCaffery's *The Friar of San Giovanni: Tales of Padre Pio*. It seemed that McCaffery – a former wartime spy master – had not only befriended Tindal in Donegal, where both had moved after the war, but they had developed a strong affection for Padre Pio. Much research and many phonecalls later, I came across what I now refer to as 'the longest trip to confession in history' involving a visit by Nicolas Tindal to Padre Pio.

'My father was a very sincere man,' Charles Tindal says of his now-deceased dad. 'He was also very spiritual and an ardent Catholic. His mother was the same before him, although his father wasn't. He got the influence from his mother. He went to Mass every day. He used to drag me to Mass, too. It was quite funny, really, because we used to have a milk round and we would go to the TB hospital in Killybegs. He used to deliver the milk to the hospital in his Jaguar Mark 10. He would then go to Mass, dragging me along with him.

'He used to go to confession, too. He thought it was very important. You can be sincere with yourself and tell people what you are really like. You are as free as air once it's over. I think he felt that way about it. He particularly wanted to go to confession with Padre Pio because he liked the idea of making a clear confession and he had heard that Padre Pio could see through people.'

In the early 1950s – around 1952, 1953 or 1954 – Nicolas Tindal and his wife travelled to San Giovanni Rotondo, where Tindal planned to have his confession heard by Padre Pio. 'They were always going off on trips, usually after Christmas,' Charles recalls, although we don't know with certainty the time of year they departed.

'They drove all the way from Donegal,' Charles explains. 'They went by ferry from Ireland, drove through Europe, into Italy and all the way down to San Giovanni, stopping at likely spots along the way to get some food and sleep. In those days it was quite a journey, but my father had been a pilot in the RAF and he wasn't worried about doing something like that. He was well able to do it.'

Knowing that Padre Pio couldn't speak English, Tindal took the precaution of meticulously writing out his confession in Italian. He hoped to read, or refer to, the document in the confessional at San Giovanni. It was a reasonable master plan, devised by a man with little or no knowledge of the Italian language. Unfortunately, the plan didn't work.

'He never had his confession heard by Padre Pio,' his son recalls. 'He was simply told, "Because you can't speak Italian, Padre Pio can't hear your confession." He was told the news by whoever was in charge at the time. I can understand what happened because Padre Pio couldn't speak English, either. It would have all been a bit difficult.

'My father was very disappointed, although I think he went to Padre Pio's Mass. He must have done, because he certainly wouldn't have gone there without doing so. They then drove all the way back through Europe and home to Donegal. I'm sure he eventually made the confession with someone else. Unfortunately, it wasn't with Padre Pio.'

That trip by Nicolas Tindal to Padre Pio in the early 1950s was the sole visit he made to San Giovanni Rotondo. He never went there again. He did remain a devotee of the future saint, however, and continued to practise his faith. He died in 2006, aged 94, leaving behind him his substantial extended family, along with the memory of an extraordinary visit to Padre Pio that, but for a chance remark by John McCaffery, might never have seen the light of day.

Mairead Doyle was one of the earliest Irish visitors to Padre Pio. She also became his close friend and set up the first Padre Pio prayer group in Ireland.

In later life, Mairead Doyle recalled how, on her first visit to San Giovanni Rotondo, she travelled on mule tracks, with mud up to her ears. Had she wished, she might also have referred to the prop planes, slow trains, battered old buses and spartan accommodation that faced pilgrims brave enough, in the 1950s, to climb into the inhospitable Gargano Mountains in the spur of Italy.

It would have been unlike Mairead to shirk a challenge like that, especially once she had discovered the mysterious powers of Padre Pio. She found out about his talents in a rather fortuitous way. 'Mairead was coming home on a bus one evening in the 1950s and she found a book about Padre Pio, written by a priest,' her niece Mary Briody explains. 'She decided, "I must go and see this man."

'She made the trek on her own; there was no such thing as organised tours at that stage. She flew to London and then to Rome. She then got a train and a bus and walked up the last bit. It was a terrible old trek, especially on your own. It was a huge ordeal just to go. Later, they said she was the first Irish girl to come up the dirt track to San Giovanni back in the 1950s.'

Mairead's first act was to visit Padre Pio's five a.m. Mass. 'She was first outside the door but when she got in she was last because the Italians just pushed her out of the way,' her niece recalls. 'The second morning they didn't push her because she had learnt.

'She was very taken with his spirituality. She said that you couldn't take your eyes off the altar during Mass. She said that his eyes seemed to penetrate through you. She made herself known and then she got an audience. She was that type of woman who would make herself known; she wouldn't just walk away. So she got in to see Padre Pio.'

By all accounts, Mairead and Padre Pio struck up a special relationship from that first meeting. From then on, she vowed to visit every year, which she did. 'She was afraid of flying and he told her that he'd always accompany her on a plane journey,' Mary Briody recalls. 'She wrote to him regularly and sent him telegrams. They were about any little thing going on in her life. It wouldn't have to be a major thing. He'd write back to her.'

She brought every member of the Doyle family to meet him over the decades. He came to know them well. He had some strange remarks to make after Mairead's parents died. On asking the friar if they were in heaven, he told her that they needed more prayer. Mairead got many Masses said. The following year, on her next visit to San Giovanni, he remarked, 'Your mamma's soul is in heaven.'

There was another peculiar instance involving Mary Briody's newborn sister, who almost died in the mid-1960s. 'When my sister Deirdre, who was the youngest in the family, was born she had three cerebral haemorrhages,' Mary remembers. 'The doctors didn't give her any hope. Daddy was told to order the white coffin. He came home and told us that the baby wasn't going to live. We said the rosary at home. Mairead had this relic of Padre Pio at the time and she put the relic on my sister and sent a telegram to San Giovanni.

'Of course, Deirdre did get better. So Mairead wrote to, or sent a telegram to, Padre Pio and said she would bring my sister over when she was four. Padre Pio's reply was, "I've already been with Deirdre." She didn't bring her over at four because Mammy wouldn't allow her, but she did bring her at eight.'

Ever since her first visit back in the 1950s, Mairead Doyle dedicated herself to popularising Padre Pio in Ireland. She travelled the country, showing films. She also set up prayer groups, the first one being established in 1970. She ran two pilgrimages a year to San Giovanni, and that was on top of her work as a lecturer in shorthand and typing in Dublin.

'She'd go down to San Giovanni on her own supposedly to look at hotels but really she just wanted to go there,' Mary Briody reflects. 'In those days the Italians weren't used to tourism. You'd often arrive and your beds wouldn't be ready. She was great dealing with that sort of thing because she took no prisoners. She would do her utmost to do everything dead right.

'She worked very hard. She was a huge organiser and she could delegate. She'd often have a Mass, say, for the tenth anniversary or something like that and, as she was a teacher, she'd have all her students helping. I'd be wondering where she got these lads with ponytails. She'd have Austin Gaffney singing. It was a huge thing and she'd do it all on her own without batting an eyelid.'

June 2002 was a special month in Rome and San Giovanni. It was a special month, too, for Mairead Doyle. After a long battle, Padre Pio was finally made a saint. 'I was with her and I shared a room with her on that trip,' Mary Briody recalls. 'She was old at the time, just a month short of her eightieth birthday.

'Even the walk up with the gift to the pope at the canonisation in Rome was a tremendous trek for her, but she was determined. That night she said to me, "Now, what will I do?" She was so happy. It was the culmination of her life's work. She was thrilled and so delighted that she had lived to see it.

'We went to San Giovanni on the next day. She went up to the tomb where there was a rosary going on. She came back to the hotel and she wasn't feeling well. We didn't think there was going to be anything wrong. She got a cup of tea and she was very hot so we got a fan. I normally went for a walk so she said, "Are you going for your walk?" I said, "No, I'm only going down for a cup of tea, I'll be up in a few minutes."' The moment Mary Briody re-entered the room, she knew Mairead was gone.

Mairead Doyle's death on Wednesday, 19 June 2002 brought to an end the life of one of Padre Pio's closest friends and greatest supporters. How ironic it was that she died in San Giovanni, just a few hours after visiting the saint's tomb. 'It was terrible for us at the time,' Mary Briody concludes. 'But, looking back, it was the best thing that could have happened.

'They put notices up around San Giovanni to say about all the work she did for Padre Pio. In Italy they put these paper notices up all around. They were in Italian with a bit in English near the end. I still have one. It was lovely. It was a glorious end after her lifetime of work.'

Padre Pio was one of the earliest advocates of the building of a basilica at Knock Shrine. His enthusiasm for the project was inspired by Gerry Fitzgerald, a Padre Pio devotee and café owner from Limerick, whose friendship with the friar began in the 1950s.

A little-known footnote to history is Padre Pio's role in the building of the Knock Shrine Basilica. His interest was aroused through his friendship with Limerick café owner Gerry Fitzgerald, who was the mastermind behind what was known as the Knock Building Project.

Having been informed of the small size of the church at Knock, Padre Pio offered, in his own words, 'grateful thanks and everlasting remembrance to all those who will help with the Knock Building Project.' He also advised Fitzgerald to contact the Most Rev. Dr. Walsh, Archbishop of Tuam, to ask for his support. The archbishop's response was in the affirmative. Even President Éamon de Valera was approached for advice.

The germ of the initiative came to life one winter during a visit by Gerry Fitzgerald to Knock. Forced to take shelter from the weather under a tree, he noticed that invalids were similarly inconvenienced and had nowhere to go. He floated the idea of building shelters to Padre Pio on one of his many visits to the friar. Padre Pio's response was enthusiastic and, once Fitzgerald returned to Limerick, a fund was set up for that purpose.

Meanwhile, the church at Knock was also clearly inadequate and required updating. The six-man committee behind the Limerick-based building project – which included Mr. D. B. O'Malley, Parliamentary Secretary to the Minister for Finance – set about the task of launching a nationwide campaign in support of a £500,000 basilica. The driving force of the scheme was Gerry Fitzgerald. Sadly, it would take until 1976 for the dream of a basilica at Knock to be realised, and by then both Padre Pio and Gerry Fitzgerald were dead.

Anyone visiting Limerick in the late 1940s, '50s and '60s might have spotted a popular eating spot on Upper Cecil Street named the Palm Grove Café. It was a novel venture for its time, 'open day and night', famous for its 'tripe and mash suppers' and selling items including eggs and bacon, steaks, chops, chips, ham, luncheons, minerals, ices, teas and coffees. 'All your food requirements' were catered for, its promotional literature claimed.

What customers may not have been aware of was the extraordinary devotion its owner, Gerry Fitzgerald, had for Padre Pio. Ever since the turn of the 1950s, he had been visiting the friar in San Giovanni, becoming his personal friend. He organised the first pilgrimages from Ireland to the stigmatic, and he continued to organise them throughout the 1950s and '60s. No one was a greater believer in, or more dedicated to, the friar of San Giovanni than Gerry Fitzgerald.

'He was a fine, respectable-looking man,' Tom Cooney, the Clare-based Padre Pio devotee who knew Fitzgerald well, told me. 'He was tall. He would talk about Padre Pio all the time. Every time we met he talked about him. In fact, there is a photograph of him sitting on a seat with Padre Pio standing over him. I used to go once a week to the café to meet him. We were personal friends and we used to be at Mass together in the Dominican church.

'He was the only man around Clare, Tipperary, Limerick and Galway who was doing these trips and is believed to be the first in Ireland to do so. About 40 people would have gone with him. Many of them would have been afraid of flying at the time. They travelled by the old planes which were smaller and not able to take the crowds they can take now. Also, you would be travelling to San Giovanni from Rome on a coach. If you had over 40 people, or so, they wouldn't be able to be carried on the coach; you'd have to get another coach and that wouldn't pay. He did seven tours, one after another.'

Fitzgerald was a master publicist, well ahead of his time. Not only was his café very well promoted, but his trips to San Giovanni and his many other ventures concerning Padre Pio received extensive publicity, too. Among those ventures was a plan to present Padre Pio with a chalice and ciborium on behalf of the Irish people. The golden chalice, of beautiful Celtic design, had an interesting history.

The chalice was on display in one of the front windows of the well-known Limerick department store, Todd's, in the late 1950s. Unfortunately, one day, the shop was gutted by fire. On hearing of the inferno, Fitzgerald arrived and spotted the chalice, rescuing it just before the building started to collapse. He felt it was destined to be Padre Pio's.

Following the publication of an article in *The Irish Press*, people from all over Ireland sent money, hoping to be associated in some small way with the gift. These spontaneous, voluntary subscriptions came from a widow with a handicapped son, a mother whose child was seriously ill and families affected by unemployment, among others.

With all this money coming in, a ciborium was purchased and £600 was set aside for the new hospital in San Giovanni. The gifts were presented to the friar on 10 October 1959. By all accounts, and from photographs of the presentation, Padre Pio was delighted and impressed. 'When I gave the gifts to Padre Pio,' Gerry Fitzgerald later recalled, 'he was deeply moved. His face lit up with a beautiful smile, and he said he would ask God to reward all those who helped in no matter how small a way.'

Gerry Fitzgerald's earthly association with Padre Pio came to an end with his death in 1967. Little over a year later, Padre Pio would be dead, too. In the following years, pilgrimages continued to leave Limerick for San Giovanni, but they were led by Tom Cooney, who is featured elsewhere in this book. The first one, which left just days after Padre Pio's death, was appropriately called the Fitzgerald Memorial Pilgrimage, commemorating one of the earliest Irish pioneers who ventured to San Giovanni and one of the closest Irish friends Padre Pio ever had.

Ireland's longest-serving religious columnist, Fr. Robert Nash, who began writing for *The Sunday Press* in 1951, met Padre Pio and observed his wounds.

Even casual readers of the now-defunct *The Sunday Press* would remember Fr. Robert Nash. Each week, from 1951 – 1985, his column appeared in the popular broadsheet, covering issues of a religious nature. At the time of his retirement, he estimated that he had produced more than a million words in what he referred to as his 'ministry of the pen.'

Following his ordination as a Jesuit in 1931, Fr. Nash was assigned as a preacher at retreats and missions. A fine writer, in 1951 he was the obvious choice to take over the Sunday religious column when the incumbent was overburdened with work. This he did with passion and fervour, never missing a week for the next 35 years. He became just as famous for his religious column as Angela MacNamara became for her advice as the paper's agony aunt.

Not long after he began his weekly feature, it was obvious to Fr. Nash that the story of Padre Pio would be of great interest to his readers. With the intention of meeting the friar, he travelled to Rome and from there by train to Foggia, eventually making his way to the nearby village of San Giovanni Rotondo. He was fortunate to meet up with two Capuchin friars on the train, who eventually secured for him special access to the inner sanctum of the friary.

Joining the friars at recreation, he found himself with the rare privilege of being in the company of Padre Pio. 'If you have the idea that Padre Pio is smug or sanctimonious in his piety, that his attitude is even remotely suggestive of the plaster saint, you are very wide of the mark,' he later wrote in *The Sunday Press*. 'A more pleasant, normally-behaved, unassuming man I have yet to meet. He chats away in the midst of a group of his brethren, is in no way averse to banter and leg-pulling, and is quite well able to give as much as he gets!'

Speaking in Latin as he had no Italian and neither did the friar speak English, Fr. Nash struck up a good rapport with the future saint. Following the established protocol, no reference was made to the stigmata, although it did cross Fr. Nash's mind that the man before him, beneath all the joviality and chatter, may be suffering the pain of Christ's crucifixion. On requesting that he might be allowed to serve Mass the next morning, the friar readily agreed.

The phrase 'lost in another world' came to Fr. Nash's mind when searching for words to describe Padre Pio during his Mass. The straightforward parts of the Mass – the Introit, Epistle and Gospel – he read at a normal pace. However, he seemed to suffer real physical distress when celebrating the sacred mysteries, resulting in many lengthy pauses. At those times, Fr. Nash said, he appeared to be experiencing the suffering of Christ on the cross.

Occasionally, as the Mass proceeded, blood oozed from one or both of Padre Pio's hands, and he used a handkerchief placed on the altar to mop it up. He prayed intensely for the living and the dead, his body and soul weighed down by the sins of those for whom he asked forgiveness. He then turned to the consecration, which lasted a lengthy 15 minutes.

Throughout the consecration, Padre Pio remained crouched over the altar, never moving, except when genuflecting. 'You experienced a feeling of awe,' Fr. Nash remarked. 'It was rather frightening to be so near, kneeling just behind, when you were convinced that the most sacred intimacies were being exchanged between God and His faithful servant.' The intimacies, Fr. Nash reflected, were not unlike those which must have taken place between Moses and God on the mountain.

No one was better positioned than Fr. Nash to observe the friar's wounds. Although not bandaged during Mass, they were covered by his long sleeves. When it came to the washing of the hands, however, a brief window of opportunity opened up. 'You can see the ugly wound, with the blood, it seems, clotted and congealed underneath a layer of skin,' he said. 'It might be an inch and a half wide. On the back of each hand there is a corresponding wound, or, rather, it is the same as the one on the palm which has penetrated.

'When he bends low over the altar, as, for instance, during the consecration, he gets into position only very gradually, moving, apparently, with difficulty and great effort. It was not till later that the probable explanation began to dawn upon me. We may not forget that in the side too he carries a wound and it is easy to understand that to bend forward, and remain in that position, may well cause him intense physical suffering.'

Eventually, after the Mass came to a close, Fr. Nash returned to the sacristy, joined Padre Pio in a prayer of thanksgiving, and began preparations for his return to Rome via Foggia. On the journey, he thought about what he had just witnessed. As the scenery passed by – the Adriatic, the olive, oak and chestnut trees, the grapes and the fields – he hardly even noticed them. Instead, his mind was occupied by images of 'that wonderful priest moving about at the altar of sacrifice,' as he put it.

He returned with these images to Ireland, imparting them to readers of *The Sunday Press* and later as part of an interesting book, *Priests*, which was published in 1961. He would go on to write other books – 28 in all – and over 300 pamphlets. Eventually, in his 80s, he retired from writing, his health deteriorated and he was finally admitted to a hospice where he spent his final days. He died in 1989, no doubt still recalling that visit to Padre Pio many decades earlier, which he always regarded as 'an experience never to be forgotten.'

Despite his extraordinary powers and charisma, Padre Pio was an ordinary, jovial, humorous man, as Corkman Donal Enright discovered on his many visits to San Giovanni Rotondo.

There were two sides to Padre Pio, according to those who knew him. Look once and you saw a supernatural, charismatic figure with piercing eyes penetrating your soul, lost in communion with God. Look twice and you saw an ordinary human being, mostly very friendly, sometimes cranky, often humorous – no different from his fellow friars apart from the bandages that covered his hands and feet.

Those two sides of Padre Pio were familiar to Donal Enright, from County Cork, who paid many visits to the friar and who became one of his personal friends. First, there was the ordinary human being: 'He was approximately 5 ft 11 in. He had large, dark brown eyes. He dressed in the brown Capuchin habit and his sandals were very large on account of the wounded feet. He wore white socks by night and brown socks by day so that people wouldn't see the blood on the white. He had a look of love on his face most of the time. Yet he could also be very frank.'

Then there was the supernatural Padre Pio, the reader of minds. Donal encountered that man, too, right from the start. He had travelled from Cork to San Giovanni a year after his mother's death. Although he had never met Padre Pio before, nor had the friar known him, the stigmatist instantly said: 'My son, you did not come here to save your mother's soul. Your mother, who is in heaven, and I brought you here to meet me.'

'I couldn't credit what I was listening to,' Donal told me. 'He had no idea of who I was and had never seen me before in my life. I was mesmerised. I felt overwhelmed, overjoyed. I kissed his hand and he saw the tears of emotion in my eyes. He just looked at me and he walked away. I will never forget it.'

On his many visits to Padre Pio, Enright saw the light side of Padre Pio. In particular, he witnessed the friar's sense of humour. It was humour characteristic of the Italian South – often described, in Padre Pio's case, as 'biting' or even 'scathing.' This characteristic was taken as evidence of the stigmatist's normality – as a psychiatrist once observed, when referring to Padre Pio, hysterical people don't normally have a sense of humour.

On one occasion, a visiting priest was the victim of a caustic remark, made in jest, not in malice. 'A priest came with a group of people,' Enright explained. 'He was an Italian priest and the Italians are often long-winded in their homilies. After Mass was over he met with Padre Pio. He said to Padre Pio, "What did you think of my homily today?" Padre Pio said, "Good, but if you kept on much longer you'd be talking to yourself." His sense of humour came through all the time.'

He could also put up with the good-natured banter of his fellow friars. Enright recalled an occasion when he was with Padre Pio's assistant Fr. Eusebio and Padre Pio arrived into their company. Cheekily, Fr. Eusebio said to Padre Pio: 'This is my most beloved friend from Ireland, kiss his hand.' Padre Pio was amused. He knew Fr. Eusebio was being funny. Enright was far from amused, however. 'I was shocked to think of him going to kiss my hand,' he recalled. He kissed Padre Pio's hand instead.

Another example of friendly banter occurred when Padre Pio was crying as he looked out the window at the hordes of people coming to see him. Enright explained how the stigmatist said, 'I don't know why they are coming here to meet me.' Fr. Eusebio responded, in an attempt to lift him up, 'I'm sorry, Father, but they are coming to meet *me*.' Padre Pio was highly amused and laughed at the remark.

Padre Pio's sense of humour was most likely inherited from his father, Grazio Mario Forgione. A poor, peasant farmer, he was born in 1860 and died in 1946. As he grew older, he moved to San Giovanni Rotondo to be close to his son. There, he was cared for by Padre Pio devotee and Irish-American heiress Mary Pyle, who was featured earlier in this book.

'One day, when his father was living with Mary Pyle in San Giovanni, some people came to meet him,' Donal Enright said, recalling an event that happened prior to his friendship with Padre Pio. 'He had a terrific sense of humour, also. He said to the people: "Padre Pio said you are to recite ten rosaries today." He later went away, chuckling to himself, as Padre Pio had said no such thing.

'That evening his father said to himself, "Oh, my God, what can I say to my son tomorrow? He'll know what I did." He didn't face him on the following day, or on the next day, or on the third day. On the evening of the third day he said, "I'll have to meet him sometime. I'll have to take whatever he says." So he met him the following day. When they met, Padre Pio was smiling. He said to his father, "It's alright this time, but never again......"'

Padre Pio also liked telling jokes, most of them innocent and redolent of their times. He would share the jokes with his fellow friars, visitors and friends. Carlo Campanini, the well-respected Italian comedian and actor, once said that Padre Pio was 'even better at that than I am.' They were always clean jokes; in the event of a crude joke being told, he walked away.

One of his favourite jokes went like this: Two old men are travelling on a train. Neither has ever been on a train before. It is daylight and they are enjoying the trip. The train suddenly enters a tunnel and everything becomes pitch black. 'What's happening? What's going on?' one of them asks. 'Maybe we're in hell,' says the other. 'Not to worry,' the first man replies, 'we have return tickets.'

There were more jokes like this, full of innocent fun, and they were all told well. The friars loved to hear them. He would, he said, 'annoy' them with the jokes, although the truth is they all wanted to spend time with him and be in his company. So, too, did those who came to visit him; no doubt they were aware of the privilege they were receiving – and the intimacy that was implied – by being the recipient of the friar's humour and not just his spiritual advice.

From his own point of view, his humour may well have kept him rational and alive. He was in constant pain from the five wounds, under pressure from his fanatical admirers, intensely involved in a complicated relationship with God, and under constant scrutiny from his superiors in the Vatican and elsewhere in the Church. With those factors alone as a backdrop, he would need all the humour he could muster to keep him sane throughout his adult life.

Mary O'Connor, from Cork, became emotionally distraught during her meeting with Padre Pio in the 1950s, mirroring the reaction of many others who met him.

When Mary O'Connor met Padre Pio in the 1950s, she was overcome by the intensity of the occasion. There was something in his eyes – a piercing, penetrating stare that seemed to burrow into her soul. There was also an aura of saintliness, implying closeness to God and contact with a world beyond human comprehension. She wasn't alone in reacting as she did, as we will see later on.

Mary first saw the friar at his confessional. 'It was amazing to witness,' she said. 'People were actually coming along and pulling his hands out of the confession box. I thought it was desperate. At times, he could be very cross, especially at Mass if he thought people weren't taking enough interest, and that's how he was that day. You could hear him giving little shouts from inside the confessional.'

Once confessions were over, Padre Pio emerged from the box, which wasn't far away. He headed straight for Mary and her child. Her husband Dan was nearby. She was mesmerised.

'He gave me his hands to kiss, he put his hands on my head and he put his hands on my boy,' she recollected. 'I looked into his face and I got an awful fright. He looked supernatural. He was different from any other living being I have ever seen. He literally shone and his eyes were remarkable. He was pale-featured, but he had a glowing expression.

'The whole thing had a huge effect on me. I was so startled that I handed over the child to my husband and I ran out of the church. I ran down the hill and I was hysterical. I worried that I had offended God all my life. I felt, "If God is anything like Padre Pio, how could I have ever offended him?"'

Some time before, her husband Dan had visited San Giovanni on his own and had reacted in a similar way. Inspired by a book he read about Padre Pio, he had travelled to see the famous friar. On that visit, he was fortunate to meet a former American soldier named Joe who knew Padre Pio and arranged for him to receive his blessing.

'Joe brought Dan to meet with Padre Pio,' Mary O'Connor recalled. 'At the time, after devotions, Padre Pio used to meet a few people who were picked out to see him. Joe took Dan to where the meetings took place and told Padre Pio who he was and where he had come from. Joe then told Dan, "Kneel down and you will get Padre Pio's blessing." That's what Dan did.

'Dan could never remember that blessing. He was so struck with Padre Pio that he just knelt down and went off into a trance. He knew that Padre Pio blessed him and put his hand on his head, but he couldn't remember anything else. Afterwards, he was completely taken by Padre Pio.'

No doubt, at the time of their experiences, the O'Connors had no idea of just how commonplace their reactions had been. Other people had also been dazzled, spellbound, transfixed by their meetings with the friar. It was not unusual for people to be left speechless or tongue-tied after their encounters. Many stories exist that illustrate this point.

One story is told of a 26-year-old Italian man, Emmanuele Brunatto, from a wealthy family, who went to Padre Pio to have his confession heard. On meeting the friar, he turned and fled, sobbing and clearly overcome by the event. He later returned and confessed, spilling out the sins of his life while experiencing the scent of roses and violets from Padre Pio.

Another story is told of an Italian, Luigi De Mercurio, who was intensely anti-religious and a disbeliever in the charisma and power of Padre Pio. He ended up in San Giovanni on business and while there, out of curiosity, decided to join a group of devotees who were about to meet the friar. Against every instinct – and defying any rational explanation – he instantly found himself kneeling before the stigmatist and kissing his habit. He could never explain why he behaved in that way.

A further story involved a Russian aristocrat, Prince Karl Klugkist, who likewise attended Padre Pio's confession. Although he didn't flee, Klugkist remarked how at the time of absolution the stigmatist became radiant with an inner light. He felt he was in the presence of the Divine. He also experienced Padre Pio's scent of perfume, which emanated from his wounds.

Despite their initial experiences, the O'Connors returned to San Giovanni on many occasions, attending Padre Pio's Masses and devotions, and watching him do christenings and weddings. 'I even remember once, after he finished his Mass, he was up in the gallery, kneeling and praying, which he often did,' Mary recalled. 'A couple were getting married and they came down the church. As they did so, Padre Pio stood up in the gallery, looked over the banister and blessed them. What a beautiful thing to do!'

In the many years ahead, the O'Connors became committed devotees of Padre Pio. They kept a photograph of him in their shop; another in their kitchen. Each time they travelled to San Giovanni, they brought hundreds of letters with them. They also fostered devotion to Padre Pio as much as they could. But, for Mary O'Connor, the event she always recalled up to her death was that extraordinary moment when she stared into Padre Pio's eyes and fled out the church door to the road outside.

'I can still see him to this day, especially his eyes and his expression,' Mary told me a few years before she died. 'There is no doubt that he was near God. He was linked to God and he was oblivious to everything else. He was, and is, a great miracle-worker. I will never forget him, especially his face on that first day I saw him. There's no way I could ever forget that. I can still see him as clearly as if he was just coming down the aisle.'

Padre Pio's 'perfume' or 'aroma of sanctity' is described in the book *Padre Pio: The Stigmatist*, which was published in 1953 and written by Irish-American Fr. Charles Mortimer Carty.

The Irish-American street preacher Fr. Charles Mortimer Carty was the first to write an English-language book about the life of Padre Pio. Published in 1953, it was called *Padre Pio: The Stigmatist*. To research the book, Fr. Carty travelled to San Giovanni Rotondo, where he lived alongside the stigmatic friar, got to know him and spoke to his colleagues in the monastery.

The book chronicles the friar's life and work, his cures and conversions, his stigmata and powers of bilocation, including his aroma of sanctity and many other features of his life up to then. It was generally well-received in the mid-1950s, becoming a recommended Christmas gift and being described as 'a fine piece of work' by the *Irish Independent*.

Not only did Fr. Carty have deep Irish roots but his life was steeped in the Catholic faith which he shared with so many other Irish-Americans. After being ordained a priest, he took to the streets with a trailer, a microphone and a loudspeaker, bringing the faith to the people rather than waiting for them to come to church. In doing so, he continued a tradition stretching back to the Apostles who street-preached throughout the Roman Empire, and to St. Francis who preached from the steps of churches, in marketplaces and from the walls of castle courtyards.

He also broadcast a radio programme *Catholic Radio Hour* in St. Paul, Minnesota, where he lived and worked. Eventually, he teamed up with an Australian priest, Fr. Leslie Rumble, who was doing similar work in his home country, and together they compiled, printed and distributed thousands of Catholic books and pamphlets in both America and Australia. It could be said that, although on a smaller scale, Fr. Carty was cut from cloth similar to that worn by the powerful outdoor preachers John Wesley and Salvation Army founder William Booth, who each brought their message to the streets.

Fr. Carty initially visited Padre Pio in April 1950 and, after attending the friar's Mass, decided to write a book on the powers and charisma of this extraordinary man. Many years before, in the early 1920s, as a seminarian in Florence, he had been told about the stigmatic by one of his professors but had never followed up by paying a visit. Following his 1950 experience, however, he vowed to return and he did so in July 1952, when he set about writing his book.

The author brought to his readers some remarkable insights concerning Padre Pio's perfume or 'aroma of sanctity'. Most often it came as a message of comfort to a person in trouble or distress, he said, although at other times it acted as a warning of impending danger or as an appeal against sin. It wasn't always a response to a cry for help; instead, it frequently arrived out of the blue. Nor was there any consistency to how long it lasted – sometimes it appeared suddenly and then vanished with speed; other times it lingered for some time. The odour could be smelled from items touched by Padre Pio.

Fr. Carty additionally noted that, as far back as 1919, Dr. Luigi Romanelli, physician-in-chief of the City Hospital in Barletta, in south-east Italy, noticed the perfume on his first visit to investigate Pade Pio. He thought it strange that a friar would adorn himself with such a fragrance. Having got the aroma again, Dr. Romanelli consulted a number of scientists. Eventually he concluded that the friar's blood not only carried the scent of perfume, contrary to the laws of science, but it could be detected by people with no sense of smell whatsoever. He also concluded that the fragrance could still be smelled even when the blood was dried or coagulated.

The aroma, we learn from the book, can vary – sometimes it is like roses; other times like violets, lilies, incense, tobacco or even carbolic acid. Sometimes it is intense; other times less so. Those who are seeking favours – people with sick children, in financial difficulties, or seeking guidance – often receive the odour, leading them to believe they are not alone, help is at hand and that their prayers are being answered.

A similar fragrance emanated from St. Lydwine, the Dutch stigmatist who had suffered all her life from illness and disease. Following an injury when she was young, she was bedridden for the remainder of her days and was stricken by numerous ailments. Having offered up her sufferings for other people's sins, it was no surprise that she became the patron saint of sickness and the chronically ill.

Lydwine's biographer, Thomas à Kempis, remarked how her room always smelled of perfume. Having initially thought it was a manufactured scent, he quickly changed his mind, noting how the aroma intensified after Lydwine received Holy Communion or following one of her visions. The hand which she claimed was being held by her guardian angel was also more fragrant. A taste of cinnamon was left in a person's mouth after experiencing it.

It wasn't Lydwine but Padre Pio that Fr. Carty was concerned with, and he ended his book with numerous depositions from people who had experienced the Italian stigmatist's redolent fragrance of sanctity. Among them was the testimony of a nun who had written to the friar asking for a favour to be granted. One night, while in bed, she was surrounded by the most delicate and aromatic scent of incense, which she immediately deduced to be from Padre Pio. She knew it was his confirmation that the favour had been granted, which indeed it had.

As with so many other examples where the grace of perfume has been detected, the impact on the nun was profound. She concluded: 'In the meantime a great peace and tranquillity have remained within me, and I feel like a child in its mother's arms. I am also aware of a sweet odour of incense which speaks to me of God, of goodness and mercy, and lifts up my soul to Heaven in an unceasing hymn of thanksgiving to my Creator for having given us mortals the good fortune to have in our midst so holy a priest endowed with such heavenly gifts.'

The following is the story of a cardinal with deep Cork roots, a pope from Poland, and the love they shared for Padre Pio. The cardinal visited Padre Pio in 1953.

In 2003, a high-powered meeting took place at the Vatican in Rome. The participants were two of the most powerful men in the Catholic Church at the time. One was Cardinal Cormac Murphy-O'Connor, who was effectively the Catholic Primate of England and Wales; the other was Pope John Paul II, who was leader of the worldwide Catholic Church.

Pope John Paul II wasn't well at the time. Aged 83, he was suffering from Parkinson's disease and was wheelchair-bound. Worn out with joint disease and still suffering the aftershock of an assassination attempt in 1981, he was in the last years of his life. Two years after that meeting in the Vatican, he would be dead.

No doubt, many issues were discussed at that formal meeting in 2003, but one of them was the hope by the visiting Church dignitary that English theologian John Henry Newman might soon be beatified. The pope stressed that evidence of a miracle would be required. Perhaps it was the issue of sainthood that prompted it, but Cardinal Murphy-O'Connor happened to mention how, during his student days in Rome, he had travelled to meet Padre Pio. The response from the pope was immediate.

Although clearly suffering from illness-related memory loss, Pope John Paul II's demeanour instantly lit up. He explained that, in his student days, he too had travelled from Rome to meet Padre Pio. The two men then went on to discuss 'holiness' – the holiness of both Padre Pio and John Henry Newman. Even towards the close of his life, Pope John Paul II had no difficulties recalling, or talking about, one of the most important events he had ever experienced – the time he spent with a friar he would later make a saint.

There hadn't been a substantial span of time between the two men's respective visits to Padre Pio. Karol Wojtyla, as Pope John Paul II was then known, had visited in 1947, while Cormac Murphy-O'Connor had arrived at San Giovanni six years later, in 1953. It was a period when the popularity of the monastery and its principal occupant was growing at a rapid pace. What had once been a place mainly frequented by locals was fast becoming a destination for foreign writers and celebrities.

Both men had been hugely impressed by the friar, and both would regard their visits as memorable moments. There are reports of how, even at that early stage, Wojtyla was singled out by Pio as a future pope. There are other reports of how the stigmatic predicted the future assassination attempt on his life. But more of that later; first to the Corkman and how his visit to San Giovanni came about.

Cormac Murphy-O'Connor's father, George, had been born in Cork, where he studied medicine at UCC. After qualifying, he departed for England and eventually set himself up in medical practice in Reading. After a time, he married another Cork person, Ellen Cuddigan, who came from Cloyne. The story of how they met is a wonderful one, recounted in the cardinal's memoirs, *An English Spring*.

Contemplating settling down, the father decided to travel to Cork to meet with a young woman he had previously fancied. Having arranged to meet in the delightful fishing village of Ballycotton, the woman arrived with her best friend. Needless to say, the friend was named Ellen, the original object of his desire was discarded, and George and Ellen were engaged within weeks! They were soon married.

Cormac was born in England in August 1932 and, while he frequently holidayed in County Cork and at Ardmore in County Waterford, the core of his life was spent in Britain. At the age of 15, he decided to become a priest, enrolling in the English College in Rome. Having completed further studies at the Pontifical Gregorian University, he was ordained to the priesthood in October 1956. It was during his studies in Rome that he travelled the long and tortuous route to San Giovanni in 1953.

Murphy-O'Connor's intention was to have his confession heard by Padre Pio, along with attending his Mass. He stayed in a hostel where he shared a room with three other students. Worried by reports that the friar could read people's souls, the four young novices spent a restless night ensuring they were omitting no sins. With one Italian-English dictionary between them, they prepared for the daunting task ahead.

First, they attended the padre's regular five a.m. Mass which, as always, was crammed with the faithful. The women shouted

'Santo! Santo!' as Pio arrived on the altar, only to be told by the friar to desist and pray. He and his fellow students witnessed the stigmata on his hands and the ecstatic state he occasionally entered, including after Holy Communion.

Unfortunately, confession was out of the question; the students hadn't anticipated the long queues. Nor did their clerical clothing prove to be of any help; no one was willing to allow them jump to the top of the line. However, they were able to meet, greet and shake hands with the future saint. That meeting, although brief, and the events surrounding it, clearly left an indelible mark on the man who would later become a cardinal of the Catholic Church.

It was to that same monastery, six years earlier, that the young Karol Wojtyla had arrived. Having only recently been ordained a priest, he is said to have remained at San Giovanni for the best part of a week, meeting with Padre Pio, attending the friar's confessional, and discussing issues of a spiritual nature. It is reliably reported that the friar told Wojtyla that he would one day wear white, meaning one day become pope. It is also said that Pio predicted that his white cassock would one day be 'stained with blood' – a reference to the subsequent attempt on his life.

Some 15 years later, an equally extraordinary event arose connecting Wojtyla with Padre Pio. It happened in November 1962, while he was Vicar Capitular of Krakow. In that month, a Polish psychiatrist and friend of the vicar, Dr. Wanda Poltawska, was diagnosed with an intestinal tumour. The prognosis was grim.

Her doctor said it was 95 per cent certain that the tumour was malignant. She was also told that, even if she survived surgery, she would have 18 months to live, at best. She had a choice to make: to go under the knife or not. With four children to rear, she opted for surgery.

Karol Wojtyla was distraught when he heard the news. He immediately wrote a letter to Padre Pio asking for prayers for his friend. On reading the letter, Pio was heard to say, 'This is impossible to refuse.' Dr. Poltawska was listed for surgery on a Friday. On the Saturday, Wojtyla telephoned her family to see how it had gone. He spoke to her husband, who informed him that she had been sent home early, before the procedure took place. Fearing the worst – that the operation had been cancelled because the tumour was inoperable – Wojtyla began to console him.

Dr. Poltawska's husband interjected, saying that it wasn't like that at all. Instead, he remarked, the doctors had discovered prior to the operation that his wife's tumour had disappeared. That's why she was sent home. 'Wanda no longer has cancer,' he explained. 'They could not find anything.'

With first-hand evidence like that as a backdrop, it was no surprise that Karol Wojtyla when he became Pope John Paul II actively furthered the case for the beatification and canonisation of Padre Pio. The first goal was achieved on 2 May 1999; the second – Pio's elevation to sainthood – came to fruition on 16 June 2002. Mind you, it was Pope Benedict XVI who eventually beatified John Henry Newman in September 2010 and not Pope

John Paul II as Cardinal Murphy-O'Connor had hoped for in his 2003 visit to the Vatican.

Looking back, it seems strange how two great men of the Church both made their way to San Giovanni at the beginning of their clerical careers. Their origins and backgrounds couldn't have been more different, yet their subsequent career paths were impressive. Both were intrinsically good men, and both shared an understanding of the importance of holiness, prayer and service to others, grounded not least on their visits to Padre Pio all those years before.

Kay Thornton and her sister Emer joined the ranks of the early Irish visitors to Padre Pio, first travelling to see him in 1955.

Travelling from Dublin to the depths of rural Italy in 1955 was little short of a nightmare. The legacy of World War II was still apparent, with bad roads, infrequent trains and inferior guest accommodation outside of the major cities. Actress Audrey Hepburn might be staying in luxury near Rome, where she was filming *War and Peace*; Argentina's great racing car champion Fangio might be living it up in Monza, where he won the Italian Grand Prix; but for the ordinary, uninitiated traveller heading to San Giovanni, the going was tough.

The most convenient train left from Rome's Central Station, Stazione Termini, at 1.34 p.m. and pulled into Foggia a little over five hours later. Ten minutes after arrival, at 6.40 p.m., the local bus left for San Giovanni and reached there after an hour-and-ten-minute drive. In the wake of a gruelling trip from Dublin, involving sea and overland travel, you would be entitled to be tired and bewildered.

That was exactly the journey undertaken by Kay Thornton and her sister Emer back in 1955. From County Dublin, neither of them had ever travelled outside Ireland before. They had been inspired by a book about Padre Pio which Emer had picked up in an aunt's house and which had been lying around at their home. After reading it, nothing could stop them from making a personal pilgrimage to see the friar of San Giovanni.

'We were immediately drawn to him,' Kay Thornton told me. 'He has this way of drawing you. We knew nothing about travelling. We were very green and were just like children. It was a very difficult trip in those days. We prayed to Padre Pio, "Look, Padre Pio, you know we are coming and you will have to look after us."

'Everything that happened was unbelievable. The people in Rome thought we were crazy; they didn't know anything about Padre Pio. When we were on the train from Rome, a young man happened to come into the carriage. He was Italian but he spoke perfect English. We were talking about Padre Pio and we told him we were going to San Giovanni. He said, "You are on the wrong train." It's hard to believe but he turned out to be a spiritual child of Padre Pio. He directed us and we arrived there safely.'

In 1955, San Giovanni Rotondo was still an old, dusty town, with very little to recommend it apart from Padre Pio. By any standards, the townsfolk were poor. Men worked as labourers in the surrounding farms, earning low wages for hard work. Some men were lucky enough to be involved in the construction of the new hospital, which opened a year later, in 1956. Construction of the new church had yet to begin; it would open in 1959.

Guest accommodation was basic, with the limited number of hotel rooms being supplemented by bed-nights in boarding houses. Although it would take a few more years for things to radically change, in the meantime, by the mid-1950s, with a growing influx of pilgrims wanting to see Padre Pio, attend his Mass, or have their confessions heard, the *raison d'être* of San Giovanni Rotondo was slowly, steadily, inexorably becoming entwined with the future saint.

'San Giovanni was very primitive at the time,' Kay Thornton reflected. 'I was very nervous and terrified of being so far away from home. It was a different era. We went to Padre Pio's Mass. We were up at the door at about half past four in the morning. The people were there in their black shawls. They were very rude to us and they just elbowed us out of the way. We were so simple; we didn't know what they were doing. They resented us. Anyway, we got in and we were right opposite the altar in the chapel. I remember him trembling after the consecration. He literally trembled. It has stuck in my mind.

'Later on, we wanted to know how to meet him. We went to the office and I said to the man, "We want to see Padre Pio. How can we do it?" He didn't speak any English but he went off and he got this American friar. He gave us two little pieces of paper, like tickets, and he said for us to come back at a certain time when Padre Pio would be passing through a corridor. He said, "You will see him then."

'We were right beside him when he walked by us. He was dressed in the ordinary brown habit with a white cord. He had this strange effect on you. We weren't able to speak. He had the same effect on a lot of people. He was a big man and he had the most fantastic eyes. I just wanted to touch him. So I touched him and he sprung around. I thought he was going to give out to me. But he never said a word. He looked straight into my eyes. I felt that he could see directly into my soul. I felt that he knew everything. His eyes were marvellous. They were big, brown eyes and they looked straight into you. There was no wavering. And that was that.'

Following their visit to San Giovanni, Kay and her sister Emer returned to Dublin, retracing the steps they had taken on the journey out. Given the insularity of Ireland at the time – and the general level of poverty – their odyssey was greeted as a notable achievement. 'Our trip was so unusual that there was a piece in the paper afterwards to say that two sisters had gone out to Italy to see this man. It was big news,' Kay recollected.

In the years to come, Kay Thornton became one of Ireland's best-known Padre Pio devotees, travelling year after year to San Giovanni and spreading his word at home. She kept a mitten of the friar, which was borrowed by people in need in numbers too numerous to mention. She also became involved in charitable work. Then, in 2013, she passed away peacefully in a nursing home, no doubt hoping to meet again the saint she so passionately revered.

Kay believed to the last that Padre Pio was one of the most special people of the twentieth century. 'There was never anyone like him before,' she told me. 'He suffered dreadfully all his life. Every single moment of his life he was suffering from those bleeding wounds and they were so sore. He must have been a special person even to survive that.

'You never forget Padre Pio. He was a profound man, like nobody I ever met. I am a very lucky person to have met him. He once put his hand on my head and that was the most wonderful thing that ever happened to me. He lets you know when you are not pleasing him and then he helps you when you do something right. He is always with you, he is always there.'

Few 'miracles' pleased Padre Pio more than the conversion of Communists to Catholicism. Dublin journalist Alan Bestic met one convert who made the switch back in the 1950s after receiving a cure from the friar.

It must have been something of a surprise to South-Dublin journalist Alan Bestic when he arrived in the town of Cerignola, 25 miles southeast of Foggia. Set on a hill, the town overlooks an extensive farm region famous for its labour agitation in the early 1900s.

At the opening of the new century, farm labourers around Cerignola were working 14-hour days in abysmal conditions, suffering from malaria and with their large families living in dire poverty. Things changed somewhat in 1908 when the labourers, who had fought for better work conditions, secured an eight-hour day.

From then on, the town and its extensive hinterland became known as 'Red' Cerignola. The local Communist Party thrived. Photos of Giuseppe Di Vittorio, the Communist politician and trade unionist, were given pride of place in people's homes. The photos would hang on walls alongside pictures of Jesus and the Madonna.

It was exactly the sort of setting that not only worried Italy's conservative elite but also caused deep concern to Padre Pio. He disliked Marxist ideology and the spread of Communism, incensed no doubt by its intense hostility to Catholicism. He advised pilgrims arriving in San Giovanni to vote against their election candidates. In fact, he would do anything he could to undermine the world's largest Communist Party outside Russia and the Iron Curtain, except for Indonesia – even using his miraculous powers, if necessary.

Alan Bestic, who had been educated in South Dublin at Kingstown Grammar School – which is now part of Newpark Comprehensive set out to find one of Padre Pio's conversion miracles for an article he was writing for the English tabloid press. His search led him first to San Giovanni where he met the friar and then to Cerignola, where he encountered a poor man named Grieco Savino. With a wife and six children, he had been a card-carrying Communist from 1945 – 1950.

It was people like Savino who had exercised the minds of Catholics in post-war Europe. Pope Pius XII articulated core Church view when he said that Communism was a doctrine 'which succeeds only in imposing on entire peoples complete slavery and the tribute of blood.' Vatican Radio reemphasised his message, declaring that 'Marxism and its political expression, Communism, are irredeemable.' The Vatican's daily newspaper *L'Osservatore Romano* added that 'the only thing which could halt Communism was the vigilance of Catholics.'

It came as no surprise when the Catholic Church announced the automatic excommunication of those who defended or who propagated the 'materialistic and anti-Christian doctrine of Communism.' The Irish hierarchy sensed the mood in Rome, with Dr. Con Lucey, Bishop of Cork and Ross, warning that Communists in Ireland were 'ready to seize power should opportunity offer in the shape of economic or political chaos, Russian aid or the like.' One Galway priest even identified the targets of Communist agents in Ireland as the Dáil, trade unions, agricultural workers and children.

The Church sent their Irish faithful into a frenzy of activity to defeat Communism. The Bishop of Ferns announced that £3,000 had been raised by Catholics in his diocese to help tackle Communism in Italy. £150 was raised in Macroom, County Cork. Between them, the Master Fish Friers' Association and the Italian colony in Dublin subscribed £250. The Bishop of Achonry took a more spiritual approach, recommending the saying of the family rosary throughout the month of April

1948. In Italy, Padre Pio approached the issue in whatever way he could, including by using his miraculous powers.

Even before he joined the Communist Party, Grieco Savino was an opponent of religion. 'I refused to allow any of my children to be baptised,' he explained to Alan Bestic. 'But in 1950 I became ill. The doctors said I had a tumour on the brain and another tumour behind the right eye. They said there was little hope. I was sent to hospital in Bari and I was afraid. That was what made me turn to God again for the first time since I was a child.'

Having been transferred to a hospital in Milan, he was told his eye would need to be removed. An operation was scheduled – a difficult one, he was informed, with the surgeon pointing out that his life 'would lie in the hands of God.' It was then that Padre Pio entered the picture.

'A few nights later, I dreamed I saw Padre Pio, who touched my head and said: "With time you will be cured,"' Savino recalled. 'When I woke up I felt much better.' Although impressed by the patient's improved condition, the doctor felt an operation was still necessary. Before it, however, he undertook one more examination of Savino. What he found shocked both doctor and patient alike.

'He turned to me in amazement and said: "I can find no trace of the tumours whatsoever." I was amazed, too, but not by what he said, for I hardly heard him. While he was examining me, you see, I noticed a strong perfume of violets and I knew Padre Pio was with me in spirit.'

Savino and his wife headed straight to San Giovanni Rotondo to give thanks to Padre Pio. Although seemingly cured of his tumours, he still complained of severe head pains. On entering Padre Pio's confessional, he raised his continuing health worries with the future saint.

'I said to the Padre: "I'm sick. I have six children. Save my life." He said to me: "I am not God. I am not Jesus Christ. I am equal with all other priests and I cannot work miracles." Then I told him: "Your habit is the same, Padre, but your heart is different. Please help me."

'For a moment he said nothing. Then he raised his eyes to heaven and began to pray. The perfume was intense. I did not understand his words, but I knew he was talking to God by the expression on his face. Then he touched my head and said: "Go to your house and pray. I shall pray in my cell and you will be cured."'

At that moment, the pain disappeared from Savino's head. He felt like weeping, but Padre Pio smiled and said: "Wherever you go, I shall go with you." He knew his illness was gone. Not only did he throw away his Communist Party membership card on his return home, but he went on to call his next child Pio after the miraculous event he believed saved his life.

Following his interview with Savino, Alan Bestic walked out into the bright sunshine of Cerignola. He wandered through its 'dismal, drab streets,' and he wondered what Savino's former Communist Party comrades thought of the man's story and his return to God. Although it was far from being Padre Pio's sole conversion of a Marxist to Catholicism – there were lots of others – it was certainly significant in this Communist Party stronghold of Cerignola.

'Here was a man who had been on the brink of death and now was healthy, a man who had known agony and was now completely free from pain,' Bestic concluded, as he reflected on the story he had only just been told. 'Even the most ardent, materialistic Party member would be hard pressed to find a natural explanation for that.'

Cork woman Margot Scannell encountered Padre Pio on four occasions. Her first, in 1956, occurred in a roundabout way.

Devotion to Padre Pio develops in many different ways. Some people inherit it from their parents or extended family; in other cases it is nurtured through prayer cards, books, pamphlets, talks, sermons, TV programmes or newspaper reports. Sometimes, people say he has come to them in dreams, with devotion developing afterwards. Other times, it follows from being blessed by a mitten or other relic in the hope of securing a miracle or cure.

Cork woman Margot Scannell's devotion to Padre Pio had a somewhat indirect, unexpected beginning. In 1956, while in hospital undergoing a hysterectomy, she was given a book on the friar. She set it aside and promised to read it at a later date, which she did. In the meantime, she had spotted a statue of St. Philomena on her way into the operating theatre. Looking up at the statue, she said, 'If I come out of this I will go to you in thanksgiving.'

She kept her promise once she recovered her health, leaving along with her husband for St. Philomena's Shrine at Mugnano del Cardinale, near Naples. 'My husband, John, was a CIE clerk,' Margot recalled. 'He had free travel and I had half travel. We went by boat and overland – Cork to Dun Laoghaire, Holyhead, London, Dover, Calais, then through France and on to Rome. It took us three days to get there and three days to get back.

'From Rome we travelled beyond Naples to St. Philomena's shrine. The next day, after seeing the shrine, we were due to go to the Isle of Capri but some people from Waterford said, "We are not going with you, we are going to a stigmatist." I said, "What stigmatist?" They said, "Padre Pio." "Oh," I said, "we'll go, I read all about him."'

On that visit to San Giovanni, Margot saw Padre Pio while he was hearing the women's confessions. He sat in the middle section of the confession box, which was open to the rest of the chapel. He remained seated there, hour after hour, with the curtains pulled aside, facing outwards, for all to see.

On Padre Pio's left was an adjoining cubicle with its top half enclosed, containing a penitent on her knees, pouring out her soul; on his right was a second semi-enclosed cubicle with another penitent waiting her turn. Outside in the chapel were crowds of women, praying, watching, staring at the friar and preparing to confess.

'He never had the curtains closed,' Margot recalled. 'The curtains would be open and you could see him. He would be looking out as well as hearing confessions. I was in the crowd. The woman from Waterford kept saying, "Do you feel his eyes on you? Do you feel his eyes going through you?" I felt I did, that his eyes were going right through me.

'Next thing, his eyes moved and they fixed on a woman near me. He called her out of the crowd and brought her up to the confession box. When that woman went up he pulled both curtains over. When the confession was over you could see the affection in the woman. She was crying. It was unbelievable.'

On her return to Ireland, Margot developed a strong devotion to Padre Pio, resulting a few years later in her making another visit to San Giovanni. This time, she experienced Padre Pio's 'aroma of sanctity'. 'I saw him passing through a room,' Margot recollected. 'I remember saying a prayer before he came in, "Lord I am not worthy that thou should enter under my roof. Only say the word and my soul shall be healed." Before he even came through the door there was a smell of ointment which went all over me. I will never forget it. I felt it was the cleaning of my soul.'

In many ways, Margot's visits to Padre Pio tracked the friar's decline into old age. This was certainly true of her third visit, in the mid-1960s. On this occasion, she had the good fortune to kiss his hand. 'Father Joseph, who helped look after Padre Pio and who I got to know, sent word down to the dining room of the hotel to say that I was wanted above,' Margot explained. 'When I went up he said, "I'll get you into this room and Padre Pio will meet you." He came into the room we were in. God help him, if you saw him trying to walk, he was shuffling along and his feet were all swollen. The priests were holding him up under his arms. He looked like a lovely old priest.

'There were only about six or eight women there. He started with the very first person and Father Joseph introduced her. He looked right through her, nothing happened between them. It came to my turn and Father Joseph introduced me. He looked right through me and never spoke either. But he put out his hand for me to kiss and then continued on. Eventually, he came to this Italian lady and he got very cross. Afterwards, I said to Father Joseph, "What happened?" He said, "She was trying to fool him." He said that Padre Pio said that why he had to speak crossly to her was because God was ready to strike her.'

Margot returned once more to San Giovanni Rotondo, this time in the month of September 1968. Her visit took place a fortnight before Padre Pio died. 'Father Joseph again got us to see him,' she said. 'That time I met him on the way down to the crypt. Father Joseph said, "Padre Pio said that when he comes out you are not to speak with your lips, you are to speak with your heart and he will know what you want." He went in for him and brought him out to the landing where you go down to the crypt. He was in a wheelchair. He looked very frail.

'He looked right through each person while they asked in their hearts what they wanted. When he had looked at every one of us, he told a priest to take his chair around and he put out his hand for us to kiss. Some he didn't touch, I'd say, because they didn't need it. But I needed it. He put out his hand for me to kiss but I couldn't get at it. Instead, he gave me a fine slap down on the head. Afterwards, I said to Father Joseph, "What did that mean?" He said, "What you asked for; he was giving you his protection."

That visit in 1968 was the last time Margot Scannell saw Padre Pio alive. By then, however, her devotion to the future saint was copper-fastened and complete. In the following years, she brought immense solace to numerous people who visited her to be blessed by a Padre Pio mitten. She also willingly recalled, for anyone who wished to listen, those four momentous visits to Padre Pio which had changed her life.

'It was great to have met him,' she concluded. 'I loved him but was afraid of him at the same time because he could read every bit of you. It was wonderful to be in his presence. He was sad to look at. You knew he was suffering. You were looking at a suffering man. Even when he was in his chair you felt he was suffering. To be honest with you, I felt that God was there; I felt it was God.'

John Coyle, from County Down, recollects how his father and aunt came to receive Holy Communion from Padre Pio in the mid-1950s.

For Padre Pio, receiving Holy Communion was the pinnacle of religious practice and belief. He once said: 'My heart feels drawn by a higher power before being united with Him in the Blessed

Sacrament. I have such hunger and thirst before receiving Him that it would take little more for me to die of longing.'

This wasn't a feeling he attributed only to himself; he also believed it should be shared by others. To paraphrase his views, how could anyone live if they failed even for a single morning to receive Jesus in communion? How could anyone not feel their chest smoulder with Divine fire at the moment they find themselves before the Blessed Sacrament?

These were exacting standards, indeed, for anyone receiving communion from Padre Pio. Many had passed the test, coming away washed with a feeling of holiness and goodliness having been, they believed, in genuine communion with God. Having had the Eucharist delivered to them by the stigmatised hands of Padre Pio brought the experience to another level.

Sean Coyle and his older sister Gabrielle received communion from Padre Pio in the mid-1950s. Unlike many others who received the sacrament in San Giovanni, they brought home a photograph to prove it. It was – and still is – a wonderful black-and-white snapshot of the moment when, kneeling before the future saint, they shared in the commemoration of the death of Jesus. The event marked the culmination of a long and arduous journey from Ireland to San Giovanni Rotondo.

'My dad Sean, who was born in 1917, and his sister Gabrielle, who was older than him, travelled to San Giovanni in the mid-1950s,' Sean's son, John, told me. 'My dad had studied the piano from a very early age and was a full-time musician. He was a concert pianist of some repute and used to give recitals and performances in Belfast. He also did some work in Dublin at the Theatre Royal.

'While he was a spiritual and religious person, his sister, my Aunt Gabrielle, was very devout. She had great devotion to Our Lady. She had been at Ardboe, in County Tyrone, when Our Lady was said to have appeared there in 1954. She was reputed, while there, to have seen Our Lady's cloak trailing along the ground. She also had devotion to Our Lady of the Hill after an apparition was said to have occurred up near Castlewellan, again in 1954.

'My dad and his sister headed off by getting the ferry to England and working their way down to Dover. They eventually got the train from France to Italy and then made their way from Rome to Foggia and on to San Giovanni. It would have been a tough trip at the time, not long after the war.

'Apparently, in Rome, my aunt was trying to ask one of the local police for directions to the bus. He started to get agitated. She took out her powder puff and was puffing her face, trying to keep his attention. Unfortunately, the powder went all over his uniform. Dad said he just wanted to climb down a drain!

'When they got to San Giovanni, they stayed in the only hotel that was there at the time. Dad's musical ability soon came to people's attention. At dinner, one day, he was given a piano-keyed accordion and was asked to play a couple of tunes. He did this and it seems they liked it. Afterwards, every time he would come into the restaurant the Italian owners would say, "The musical maestro!"

'Eventually, my dad received Holy Communion from Padre Pio. The occasion is recorded in a black-and-white photo. You can see Dad in a heavy coat and wearing a scarf and a white shirt, with dark, neat hair and his mouth open, receiving the communion on his tongue. In the photo, Padre Pio is distributing it with his right hand and you can make out the mitten quite clearly.

'Gabrielle is kneeling on Dad's left. She is wearing a hat with a veil and is looking very devout. There is an extraordinary look of love on her face. However, the centrepiece of the photo is Padre Pio, who looks very peaceful and compassionate. We still have the photo to this day.'

While in San Giovanni, Sean and his sister participated in all the other priestly activities of Padre Pio including, in Sean's case, the blessing of his proficient hands. 'He really had a remarkable touch with his hands and they meant a lot to him,' John Coyle said. 'He was, after all, a concert pianist and he taught piano as well. The blessing must have pleased him a lot.'

The family's musical aptitudes would again feature, many years later, during a further visit to San Giovanni but this time involving Sean's sons John and Patrick. Initially, John had paid a visit on his own, 'probably to make the same journey my dad had made,' as he put it. 'I felt drawn to where he had gone and also to Padre Pio. It was just something I wanted to do.' The two brothers then embarked on a second visit – and that's where music entered the picture.

'On that second trip, my brother Patrick was with me,' John recollects. 'He is also a concert pianist, just like my dad was. When we were there, in our hotel, some of the pilgrims we were with knew of his musical talent. They asked him if he would play the piano for them. That's what he did. He gave an impromptu recital in the lounge of the hotel, to the delight of the pilgrims and hotel staff. It was reminiscent of what had happened with my father all those years before.'

During both visits, John Coyle never got to see the body of Padre Pio. On the first visit the Capuchins were undertaking renovations to the display area and access to the body was being temporarily denied; on the second trip the body was no longer on view and had been reinterred in a sealed casket. 'So, unlike my dad, I never saw Padre Pio,' John remarked. Back home in County Down, however, there still was that wonderful black-and-white photograph of his father and aunt at communion, and the treasured memories of their visit in the mid-1950s.

'I was a bit disappointed that I never saw Padre Pio, but maybe he had a reason why that should have been,' John reflected. 'However, my dad's visit is still recalled in our family. We talk about it when we're together. It might come up in conversation. On those occasions, we remember how my dad and my aunt made their pilgrimage to San Giovanni to see Padre Pio over half a century ago.'

Irish woman Mary Ingoldsby spent much of her life in Italy. During her time there, she came to know Padre Pio and wrote an extraordinary book on his life.

Italy was hit by a wave of bitterly cold weather in 1956. The cold spell was nothing short of historic. Freezing winds and blizzards packed with raw, icy snow poured from the Arctic down throughout Europe, crippling Rome and isolating rural villages. Lakes froze, roofs collapsed, snowflakes as large as handkerchiefs were reported; even the long-awaited Roma – Lazio football derby in mid-March was postponed due to heavy falls of snow.

Nowhere was this nasty 'Snowfall of the Century' more dramatically felt than in mountain outposts like San Giovanni Rotondo, high up in the Gargano Mountains. The friars there had a lot to lose from the inclement conditions. In May, the new hospital and Padre Pio's brainchild – Casa Sollievo della Sofferenza – was scheduled to open. Construction would also soon begin on the new church of Santa Maria delle Grazie to cater for the flood of people coming to see Padre Pio.

It was into this dramatic setting of bitter cold, energetic construction and uncharacteristic change that an Irish woman, Mary Ingoldsby, arrived for her first encounter with Padre Pio. Then in her early 40s, she had reached this life-affirming moment through a long and interesting route. Born in Dublin in 1914, she had worked as a civil servant in Ireland before eventually departing for Italy, where she took up religious studies in Rome.

Arriving in Italy in 1939, as the country teetered on the brink of war, she eventually worked at various jobs including translator for a number of Vatican departments and as assistant to the U.S. Bishops' Press Panel. Other jobs included Legion of Mary envoy to Italy, a capacity she worked in from 1946 – 1958. At the time, the Legion of Mary – founded in Dublin in 1921 by Frank Duff – was spreading its power base far and wide. In the 1960s, she also wrote a Rome Letter for *The Irish Press*.

It was inevitable that Ingoldsby would refer to the bitter cold of 1956 as she set out to climb the steep hill from the village to the friary for Pio's five a.m. Mass. That walk, she said in her book *Padre Pio: His Life and Mission*, published in 1978, was a penitential rite all by itself. Despite the weather, local women were already jammed up against the church door, waiting to get in. Once the door was opened, they became frantic and unruly in their efforts to gain the best vantage spots near the altar. Only when Padre Pio arrived did silence descend on the congregation.

Padre Pio was clearly in great pain as he ascended the altar on his perforated and bleeding feet, Ingoldsby observed. His washed-out, pained face, she said, was like the face one imagined had belonged to Christ struggling with the weight of his cross. Driven by curiosity, once the Mass had ended she walked over to where the padre had knelt and discovered little cushions underneath the carpet at places when he was required to move during his Mass. Despite their presence, he had shuffled with difficulty, the soreness from his wounded feet notably causing severe discomfort.

Ingoldsby obtained from others, mostly people the friar had directly spoken to, a more precise insight to the intensity of his Mass. Pio had explained, on different occasions, how during Mass he offered himself as a victim for men's sins, suffered greater pain than at any other time during his day, was able to remain standing only in the same way that Jesus remained upright on the cross, and died each Mass not out of pain but love.

The Irish woman also observed how many people remarked that, after the consecration, he seemed to turn into Jesus himself. During the prayers for the living and dead, when he prayed for his 'spiritual children' and those who had departed, he was completely absorbed in the task at hand. Before his communion, while proclaiming 'Lord, I am not worthy,' he beat his breast with such force that one wondered how either wounded hands or chest could withstand the force.

She also documented some extraordinary miracles and cures. One of the cures concerned a priest who had grown seriously ill from liver disease and who was a former fellow novitiate of Padre Pio's. One night, in 1957, while in his hospital bed, he was visited by Padre Pio who conversed with him and advised him to have patience. The friar then disappeared via the window, having first placed his hand on the glass.

The following morning, the imprint of Pio's hand was still on the glass and, for many days afterwards, each time it was rubbed off it reappeared. Padre Pio was later queried about whether he had paid some sort of extraordinary visit to the priest; he certainly hadn't physically left the monastery and done so in person. 'Do you doubt it?' Padre Pio replied, in the typically mysterious manner he frequently used. The ill priest made a full recovery.

Mary Ingoldsby eventually spent a significant part of her life in San Giovanni Rotondo, primarily in the 1970s after the friar had died. She remained there for almost two years translating into English the first volume of his letters to his spiritual directors. She also spent time at the village investigating the stigmatic's mysterious talents and abilities, talking to his former colleagues and publishing her subsequent insights and conclusions in her 1978 book.

In her later years, she returned to Ireland, residing for a time at the Rosminian House of Studies, based in Clonmel, County Tipperary. There, she translated major writings of the founder Rosmini, who was one of the great theologians of the nineteenth century. She also wrote a book about him, drawn no doubt by his reputation for holiness – something he shared with a man she had met many years before.

In April 1994, aged 80, Mary Ingoldsby died in County Meath. Although still known for her book on Padre Pio, her remarkably important role in the life of the friar is often overlooked and is frequently forgotten. It cannot be denied, however, that in 1939, when she left on her long adventure to Italy, she became one of those pioneering, determined women who marked themselves out as very special people and, in Mary's case, as one of the early discoverers of the saintly and charismatic powers of Padre Pio. She was an extraordinary woman, indeed.

Actress Diana Graves, the niece of poet Robert Graves, whose father in turn was the Dublin-born Anglo-Irish poet, songwriter and folklorist Alfred Perceval Graves, met Padre Pio in the mid-1950s. She had travelled to meet him in the hope of a cure for her chronic lung ailments.

While working as an actress in the late 1940s and at the turn of the 1950s, Diana Graves harboured an untreatable disease that was severely curtailing her life. A sufferer from two serious lung conditions – one being emphysema; the other involving damage to the wall of her bronchial tube – she found it difficult to breathe, her heart was overworked, and she faced being an invalid for the rest of her life.

The advice she received was simple and clear – move to a warm, dry climate if you wish to survive. Many destinations were considered, but she settled on Rome. Her choice was partly because her cousin Jenny already lived there and also because she might get some work at Cinecittà, the famous Italian film studio which had been established by Mussolini in 1937 and, by the time of Diana's decision to move there, had become known as Hollywood on the Tiber.

In Rome, things didn't quite work out as planned. Her illness and its symptoms continued to impair her life. Acting work was difficult to come by, although she did secure employment for a time as a dubbing director. She also befriended the Irish author Kate O'Brien, who had moved there, along with O'Brien's close Irish friend and academic Lorna Reynolds. Another friend who visited Rome for a time was the Irish-British screenwriter and playwright, Bridget Boland, who wrote the screenplay for *War and Peace* (1956). Together with them, she made the best of her time in the Italian capital.

Worn down by her illness, and clearly not recovering, it was suggested to Diana that she might consider travelling to a village near Foggia where a man called Padre Pio was effecting miraculous cures. This man, she was told, was a saint and the personification of goodness. Although not a believer in miracles, she decided to travel to San Giovanni the following weekend in the company of her cousin.

The sight that greeted their arrival surprised them both. The village was deserted, the rain drizzled down, not a soul was in sight. Enquiring of their driver why things were so quiet, they were told that everyone was in the church because Padre Pio would soon be hearing confessions. Although feeling tired and unwell, Diana entered the packed, airless church, where she leaned against a pillar to stop herself from fainting.

Suddenly, a loud commotion erupted and the crowd swept forward towards the altar. Their arms were outstretched as they begged the figure that had emerged for a blessing. Others tried to touch his robes. The church throbbed with emotion. What sort of man could this be, Diana wondered, who was able to transform so many poor peasants into a simmering, bubbling mass of devotion on a daily basis?

She watched as he entered the confession box, where he sat with the curtains open, his head leaning out, and a look of pain on his face. One of his stigmatised hands grasped the side of the door with such force that he seemed to be penetrating it. There he sat, for two hours, listening to the sins of the penitents, looking tired and distressed but exuding a fierce compassion. The image of the tears and sighs of the many sinners, and their indistinct confessions, was emblazoned on Diana's mind.

Later, Diana encountered one of Padre Pio's English-speaking colleagues, Fr. Domenico, who agreed to secure admission for her to the sacristy, where she might receive the future saint's blessing. Crowds of people were congregated outside, jostling and shoving, and trying to gain entry. Inside, around 12 people awaited the padre's arrival. Diana was worried, having heard that he could see into people's souls and dismiss those he felt lacked goodness.

Although feeling weak and shaking with fear, she remained in the sacristy until Padre Pio arrived. Having been prompted by Fr. Domenico, the padre at first stared at Diana with piercing eyes then walked towards her with a compassionate smile on his face and with his hand outstretched. She knelt and kissed it. He then placed his other hand on her head and blessed her, before departing the room.

Suddenly, people crowded around her, suffocating her and pressing their faces against hers. Alarmed, she asked her cousin what they were saying. Contrary to her fear that they were threatening her, she was told that they were saying she had received a special blessing and she would get well. Overcome with emotion, Diana burst into tears. The others cried, too, helped her up from her knees, and placed their arms around her.

Arising at three o'clock the following morning, Diana and Jenny attended Padre Pio's early-morning Mass. Once again, the church was packed and the crowd unruly. Padre Pio arrived, telling people to be quiet, sweeping them aside and ordering them to respect the house of God. During the consecration of the host, he faced the congregation with tears streaming down his face.

Diana and her cousin Jenny eventually travelled back to Rome, overcome by their short visit to San Giovanni. It was, Diana felt, the most extraordinary experience ever. Never had she encountered someone with such goodness and spiritual strength. Nor had she ever before been in the presence of anyone exuding such peace and comfort. Should they be the qualities that make a saint, she mused in her book, *To My Astonishment*, published in 1958, then, so be it, Padre Pio was clearly a saint.

The widow of radio pioneer and Nobel Prize winner, Guglielmo Marconi, who had extensive Irish connections, not only met Padre Pio but was present in 1956 for one of the most important days of his life.

Fifteen thousand people flocked to San Giovanni Rotondo for the inauguration of Padre Pio's recently-built, state-of-the-art hospital, which saw the first light of day on 5 May 1956. He had dreamed of building the Casa Sollievo della Sofferenza since the mid-1930s. Now, 20 years later – on a day blessed with bright skies and clear sunshine – the work was finally completed and the hospital was unveiled to the world.

It seemed that everyone had arrived for the event. Press photographers, reporters and newsreel cameras were there to record the occasion. Bishops, archbishops and dignitaries from Italy and elsewhere were present. President of the Italian Senate, Cesare Merzagora, and Minister Giovanni Braschi, represented the government. Fr. Benigno, Minister General of the Capuchins, came, too. Cardinal Lercaro, Archbishop of Bologna, introduced proceedings. Padre Pio spoke movingly and eloquently; he also said an open-air Mass.

Not everyone would have recognised the two distinguished guests standing in pride of place as the ceremony proceeded. Both were well-known to Padre Pio and the friars at San Giovanni. One was Maria Cristina Marconi, widow of the late Guglielmo Marconi, the radio inventor and pioneer who had many strong Irish connections. Beside her, on her left, was her daughter Elettra, aged 25. Both were dressed conservatively for the occasion. Maria Cristina held a rosary beads in her hands.

Maria Cristina Marconi was a member of the Bezzi-Scali family, who were part of the Roman aristocracy and fervent Catholics. They lived in a baroque palazzo near the Spanish Steps in Rome. She was Marconi's second wife, marrying him in June 1927. It was an elegant wedding, with the reception taking place at the Bezzi-Scali family residence. For the occasion, the bride wore an interesting piece of Irish lace that had belonged to Marconi's mother – and therein hangs a fascinating tale.

Although Marconi is forever recognised as an 'Italian' genius and radio innovator, his mother's family had originally hailed from County Wexford in Ireland. The family name was Jameson. They were famous for their Jameson whiskey – producing over one million gallons a year by the 1800s from their Bow Street distillery in Dublin.

The Jameson family lived in Montrose House, which can still be seen in the grounds of the Radio Telefís Éireann broadcast centre in Dublin. Eventually, one of the girls, Annie, married Marconi's father, having met him in Bologna where she was sent to study at the music conservatory. The marriage took place in 1864. Their son, Guglielmo, was born ten years later, in April 1874.

There were interesting conflicts in the inventor's religious background, with his father being an Italian Catholic and his mother Annie being staunchly Protestant. Annie was determined that her family would not be educated by priests. As a result, while Guglielmo was baptised as a Catholic he was brought up as a Protestant. This didn't seem to affect him in future years when he befriended popes and became an important contributor to the development of the Vatican's communications network.

Marconi's Irish connections were even more pronounced than the nationality of his mother. Throughout his career, he established eight radio transmission stations in Ireland, including in Clifden, County Galway, and in Crookhaven, County Cork. He also married an Irish woman – the Hon. Beatrice O'Brien, daughter of Lord Inchiquin of Dromoland Castle, which today is run as an exclusive hotel. They married in March 1905 but the marriage was annulled in April 1927. Two months later, he married Maria Cristina in a civil ceremony and later in a church in Rome.

Prior to their marriage, Maria Cristina inspired Guglielmo to convert to her religious faith, Catholicism. She advised him to study the New Testament and to read the famous religious classic *The Imitation of Christ*. He was particularly impressed by the writings of St. Paul and St. Augustine. The inventor eventually received the sacrament of confirmation at Maria's family palace in Rome, with her father Count Bezzi-Scali as godfather.

It was also Maria Cristina who introduced Marconi to the Vatican at the highest-possible level. Since his youth, Pope Pius XII had been a family friend of the Bezzi-Scalis and had even given catechism lessons to Maria Cristina. Through her, the inventor received a welcome introduction. More importantly, he had been introduced to the previous pontiff, Pope Pius XI, who took a great interest in his research.

Maria Cristina describes in her book *Marconi My Beloved*, written with her daughter Elettra, how Pope Pius XI was always happy to receive Guglielmo and herself in private audience when they visited Rome. The visits were prolonged. 'We used to come out of His Holiness's study after two or three hours, sometimes at three in the afternoon to the dismay of the gentlemen of the court and the various prelates in waiting who were hungry for their lunch,' she wrote.

It was at one of those audiences, in 1930, that Pope Pius XI asked Marconi to set up a radio station in the Vatican to enable the pope's voice to be broadcast throughout the world and to ensure that everyone could receive his blessing Urbi et Orbi. The result was Vatican Radio, which was inaugurated in February 1931, becoming the world's first major broadcast propaganda vehicle and inspiring Adolf Hitler to set up a replica to further his own political ends.

It is not recorded if Guglielmo Marconi, during the years up to his death, met Padre Pio. What we do know, however, is that his second wife, Maria Cristina, did meet with him and was sufficiently well-regarded to be invited, along with her daughter, as an esteemed guest to the opening of the hospital in 1956.

Just like Beniamino Gigli, the famed opera singer who was a significant contributor to the funding of the hospital, it is reasonable to speculate that Maria Cristina Marconi may well have made contributions, too. She was obviously a woman of means, not only coming from the wealthy Italian family the Bezzi-Scalis, but also by being, along with her daughter, the sole beneficiaries in Marconi's will. It surprised many that he made no provision in his will for his first wife, Beatrice, and the family they had produced together.

Either way, Maria Cristina turned up for that fateful day in 1956 when the hospital was finally inaugurated after a 20-year struggle to find its feet. She was given an honourable mention in – and action shots of her and her daughter appear in – the historic Italian newsreel recorded at the event. They show her as concentrated in prayer, reverential and intensely devout.

Perhaps in those shots she was recalling her former husband, Guglielmo Marconi, who had died 19 years beforehand. Their marriage, she once wrote, had been a 'truly happy and Christian' one. The lead-up to his death had been a Christian one, too. A few days before he expired, he had visited the pope at Castel Gandolfo. Before departing, he had asked for a special blessing 'in case I would soon need it.' And need it he did. He died three days later, on 20 July 1937.

Dr. Paul Dudley White, the world-famous heart expert from the 1950s and '60s who had strong connections with Ireland, also attended the inauguration of the hospital.

There is a wonderful story told by Padre Pio devotee and author John McCaffery about the American heart specialist Dr. Paul Dudley White. The reliable McCaffery witnessed the event, establishing its authenticity. It happened during the international medical conference that followed the opening of Padre Pio's dream hospital, Casa Sollievo della Sofferenza, in May 1956. Dr. White was without doubt the most famous clinician who attended the prestigious gathering.

On the Sunday – the day following the hospital's inauguration – a reception was held for the medical experts in the friary. Padre Pio made a speech, thanking them for coming, congratulating them on their achievements and, as he so often did, remarking that they should care for people's souls as well as their physical bodies. It was a courteous, respectful speech, the highlight of a warm, positive gathering and a tribute to those who had arrived from far and wide.

Dr. White, who was a kind and mannerly man, was clearly upbeat and enthusiastic, energised by the occasion, perhaps even overcome by the enormity of what was taking place in the company of a person as special as Padre Pio. As McCaffery observed, the doctor kept taking photographs of the friar and bumping up against him. The unfortunate punchline of the story then ensued. As Dr. White said his goodbyes to the future saint, he found himself stuck for words. All that came out was the hapless remark – 'And, Father ..... congratulations on your wounds!'

We do not know the reaction of Padre Pio, who probably didn't understand what was being said as he wasn't competent in English. Although the remark would have been translated for him by a fellow friar, he most likely dismissed it as the utterance of a nervous, kindly man. He would also have known, of course, that the comment was made by a clinician who was regarded as the world's greatest medical heart expert and an international celebrity in his own right. It is difficult to comprehend today just how well-respected and well-known Dr. White was at the time.

In 1955, Dr. Paul Dudley White became famous throughout the world for his role as President Eisenhower's physician during his serious heart attack in the autumn of that year. His involvement in bringing the president back to good health was covered by the media everywhere, including in Ireland. His association with Ireland would blossom in the decades ahead – as a speaker at many conferences and events, as a popular guest on *The Late Late Show* on Telefís Éireann, as a supporter of the Irish Heart Foundation, as a guest of Taoiseach Éamon de Valera, and as a visitor to County Mayo where he loved to go fishing.

He also became an international advocate for many of the measures concerning the prevention of heart disease that we take for granted today. A firm believer in exercise, he once remarked: 'Keep active all through life. Don't gain a pound in weight after 22, and don't smoke.' Smoking, he said – and this was at a stage when it was not a popular or common remark – can damage those with any amount of heart disease and 'can cause cancer of the lungs.' Tobacco, he concluded, 'is terrible.'

Again, contrary to the conventional wisdom often articulated at the time, he dismissed the role of hard work in heart disease. 'It is not the stress and strain of modern life, but the fact that people neglect their health that causes heart disease. Hard work never hurt anyone,' he commented. He added, on another occasion, with a mischievous smile: 'Stress and strain started in the Garden of Eden and has not ended since.' Nor were our ancestors immune to stress, especially when they emerged from their fortresses to repel raiders. 'Was there not a great deal of stress and strain involved there?' he asked.

Dr. White also took a great interest in the progression of heart disease in Ireland, pointing out, in 1966, that there was an 'appalling frequency' of cardiac illnesses of many kinds in the country. On the other hand, he headed up a study comparing heart disease among Irishmen living in Ireland and their brothers living in Boston. The study showed that Irishmen living the comparatively plush life of the Boston area tended to have higher blood pressure than their harder-working kin on the west coast of Ireland. The Boston-Irish also tended to be heavier and to have more fat in their blood. The conclusion, he said, was that 'the push-button life led by so many Americans is not a good thing.'

Dr. White had many remarks to make about Padre Pio, too, saying in particular that he was 'deeply impressed' by the work he had done in bringing into existence the new hospital at San Giovanni. He was especially taken with the padre's philosophy that the hospital's purpose should be to alleviate the suffering of both body and soul – 'a place of prayer and science where human beings should meet one another in Christ,' as the friar put it. 'This clinic, more than any other in the world, seems to me to be more adapted to the study of the relationship which runs between the spirit and the sickness,' Dr. White concluded.

Once back in America, following his visit to San Giovanni in 1956, the frail, silver-haired Dr. Paul Dudley White continued his pioneering work up to his death in 1973. Riding his bicycle every day, and exercising continually, while also using a new-fangled pedometer to see that he got in enough walking, he tirelessly promoted the case for physical fitness to stem the advance of heart disease. He also became heart consultant to

U.S. President Lyndon B. Johnson and acted as President of the International Cardiology Foundation.

What was less known was that he eventually converted to Catholicism and helped raise funds in America for Padre Pio's Casa Sollievo della Sofferenza. Clearly, he never forgot the impact of that visit to San Giovanni and his meeting with the future saint. But then again, Dr. White was a man of many treasured memories – he also never forgot his days fishing around Westport, in lovely Clew Bay. It is no surprise to discover that he lived a rich, full, active life and – following his own medical advice – survived to the ripe old age of 87.

Lauri Duffy travelled from Ireland to San Giovanni Rotondo in September 1957, just as the number of pilgrims visiting the friar had grown to unmanageable proportions.

September was invariably one of the busiest months in San Giovanni Rotondo in the 1950s. Perhaps it had something to do with the weather. The Italians avoided the hot months of July and August and saved their pilgrimages for the onset of milder weather in September. They liked May and June, too, but it was September that brought the arrival of busloads, and even truckloads, of pilgrims intent on catching sight of Padre Pio.

Travellers from abroad also favoured the balmier end-of-summer weather. They, too, arrived in droves. The pressure on the friars was so severe that, by 1956, they were already building a new church to cater for the hordes of people. It wouldn't be completed until 1959. In the meantime, the tiny old chapel of

Santa Maria delle Grazie, next to the monastery, had to cater for the everyday crush.

When Lauri Duffy travelled to San Giovanni in 1957, the congestion problem was at its peak. It was so bad that Mass had to be said at a temporary altar set up outside the monastery. It was to this makeshift structure that the faithful defied the morning chill and wound their way up the steep hill to attend Padre Pio's five a.m. Mass.

'Mass was being said in the open outside the monastery to accommodate the huge number of pilgrims,' Lauri Duffy later recalled in an article written for *The Irish Press*. 'Abruptly at five o'clock the chattering and shuffling of those waiting ceased when the aged priest appeared. He commenced Mass immediately. Now the only sound was the murmured prayers of the priest and server. Nobody seemed to mind the biting cold wind. Everyone's attention was fixed on the bearded stigmatist who is believed to relive Christ's passion while celebrating the Holy Sacrifice.'

Already, by 1957, Padre Pio was 70 years old and suffering from many health issues which affected his daily life. He had always suffered from breathing problems associated with his asthma and bronchitis, and they hadn't gone away. He also experienced stomach pains and the onset of arthritis. Then, of course, there was the continuous pain from his wounds, which caused considerable discomfort especially while saying Mass.

'His every movement appeared to be painful,' Lauri Duffy recollected. 'When he genuflected it seemed as though a heavy cross weighed him down. He rose with great effort. When he turned towards the congregation and extended his hands the reddish brown scabs on his palms were plainly visible. Many gasped when they saw these marks for the first time.'

Duffy also remarked how a trickle of blood from the wounds on his hands could be seen by those close to him – a phenomenon that could only be witnessed during Mass as he always wore mittens at other times of the day. Reflecting almost all other accounts, Duffy likewise observed how time passed by quickly even though the morning Mass never took less than an hour and a quarter. 'The atmosphere was so absorbing throughout that the hour and a quarter had passed almost as soon as it had begun,' Duffy reflected.

At the time of Duffy's visit, Padre Pio continued to perform all his regular duties even though he was still absorbed in the new hospital which had opened only the year before. Apart from his priestly obligations, especially the hearing of confessions, he also met, greeted and blessed specially-selected pilgrims who had come to see him. Lauri Duffy was lucky enough to become one of those privileged individuals, receiving a genuinely joyful, spontaneous welcome from the friar.

'My meeting with Padre Pio, entirely unexpected, was the highlight of my visit to San Giovanni Rotondo,' Lauri commented. 'Shortly after my arrival I met a member of the hospital staff who had visited Ireland. We struck up a friendship. One day we gained admittance to the monastery and guided by one of the other monks waited in a corridor along which Padre Pio would pass on his way to the church.

'In due course he approached us, whereupon the monk stopped him and introduced me as a visitor from Ireland who would like his blessing. "Ah! Un Irlandese!" he beamed, and with that he gave my forehead a hearty tap with his right hand. He allowed me to kiss his hand and then beckoned to me to kneel while he gave me his blessing. Then he went on his way.'

Following the visit to San Giovanni, Lauri Duffy returned to an Ireland which, just like Italy, was still on its economic knees. In 1957 alone, two per cent of the Irish population – some 60,000 people – emigrated. Growth was non-existent, standards of living were drastically low, and Éamon de Valera had recently declared that Fianna Fáil's 'greatest national objective' was the restoration of the Irish language.

For Lauri Duffy, however, the gloom was counterbalanced by the visit to that 'amazing man' in San Giovanni who, for almost 40 years up to then, had borne the marks of Christ's wounds. Meeting him had been the highlight of Lauri's life. 'Our meeting could not have been shorter,' Lauri concluded. 'But it will remain, nonetheless, my most treasured memory.'

Christmas held a special place in the heart of Padre Pio from his childhood to his death.

In 1959, Padre Pio sent a letter to his Irish benefactors wishing them a happy Christmas. The letter was channelled through Gerry Fitzgerald, the Limerick devotee who organised the earliest Irish pilgrimages to San Giovanni Rotondo. He, in turn, had it published in the press. At the core of the letter was a very simple sentiment offering to his Irish followers 'an incessant flow of blessings' and wishing them 'a very happy Christmas and a prosperous New Year.'

The message was a warm, thoughtful one, especially coming as it did from Padre Pio. No one adored Christmas more than him. It was his favourite time of the year. The story of the Nativity, where the baby Jesus was born in a stable in Bethlehem, bringing God into people's lives and light to the world, often moved him to tears. 'In the end, the gamble of our life is all in this Child,' he used to say.

His superior at the friary in San Giovanni Rotondo wrote in his diary shortly after Padre Pio received the stigmata in 1918: 'He counts the days to go from one Christmas to the next. He thinks about it all the time. The baby Jesus holds a special attraction for him. It is enough for him to hear a Christmas carol or a lullaby and his spirit soars.'

As a young boy, Padre Pio loved preparing the crib, often constructing it many months in advance. Coming from a very poor family, he would mould clay from the fields into miniature shepherds, animals and other crib figures. He always took extra effort with the baby Jesus, making sure he was right. He would also put oil into little shells and use them as tiny lanterns to light the crib.

His midnight Mass at Christmas was renowned. Although the superior would normally be assigned this Mass, the privilege of celebrating it was always given to Padre Pio. People would travel to it on their donkeys and carts up the old dirt-track to the friary, which would often be icy or covered in snow.

In the church that night, Pio would raise the figure of the baby Jesus to the congregation and bless them with it. He would then put it in the crib. The place would be filled with the sounds of Christmas carols and other hymns. Although people would be freezing, everyone would sit there, enraptured by this extraordinary friar as he celebrated another cold night long ago when the baby Jesus was born.

In my own research, many of Padre Pio's miracles and cures were associated with Christmas and the festive season. One man – an Irish priest – related the story of a four-year-old girl with leukaemia who was due to go to hospital during Christmas week for a check-up after extensive treatment with chemotherapy. He prayed for her to Padre Pio; her family prayed, too.

'I remember one Sunday, just before Christmas, the mother and child were in the back of the church and it was cold,' Fr. Tom told me. 'The child had lost her hair. Her younger sister jumped up into my arms and was talking to me. She said, "Fr. Tom, aren't those roses something special?" I couldn't smell any roses, but the child could.

'The mother said, "Stop talking nonsense. It's Christmastime and there are no roses." The girl started to cry and said, "But it's all around us." I began to go weak at the knees. I thought, "Padre Pio is here!"

'The mother then said she was going to Dublin the next day. I said, "Give me a ring when you're up there." I don't know why I said that, but I really felt something was going to happen. And it did. They did the usual tests at the hospital the next day and the specialist said to the mother, "There's no leukaemia in that child!" The child was fine.'

Another Christmas story concerned a baby who was born with a malformed heart, containing a single ventricle instead of two and only three chambers instead of four, along with a grossly-enlarged liver. Born three weeks before Christmas, she was given no chance of survival. As Christmas approached, the mother was told to take her home. 'The nurses were in tears when we were carrying her out on Christmas Day,' the baby's mother, Ann, told me. 'However, the doctor who gave me medication and prescriptions reiterated, "Your baby isn't going to live."'

Four years passed by and the girl was still living, yet the family were again told the girl was going to die. That length of time – four years – was the most any child with her condition had survived, the mother was informed. On her fourth birthday, however, following prayers to Padre Pio – and a remarkable vision of the friar reported by the girl – the news from a crucial check-up in Dublin was startling.

The girl's heart was completely normal; she had two ventricles instead of one; her liver was reduced in size. Ann recalled the conversation with the doctor, who said: 'You can take her home, she's absolutely perfect. You've got a miracle and I don't know how you got it.' Ann also vividly remembers her response: 'I said, "I know exactly where I got it from!" After that, I rang everybody and told them what had happened. When I told my mother, she said, "I told you that Padre Pio wouldn't let you down!"'

Donegal resident and Padre Pio's friend, John McCaffery, also came across a Christmas miracle. He described how, when travelling by train from Rome to Foggia, he encountered an American woman who was in the depths of depression and despair. They started chatting. As the train entered a tunnel, she compared her life to the sudden darkness. Her only glimmer of light, she said, was Padre Pio, who she was on her way to see.

Her visit to San Giovanni transformed her life. Padre Pio was informed of her story shortly after her arrival. That same day, she experienced his perfume of roses or 'aroma of sanctity'. During her stay, although a lapsed Catholic, she undertook extensive contemplation and prayer. Eventually, both she and McCaffery went their separate ways.

Shortly after Christmas, a letter dropped into McCaffery's letterbox back in Donegal. It was from America and dated Christmas Eve. The woman explained in the letter how she was about to go to midnight Mass and receive Holy Communion for the first time in 11 years. She had emerged from her tunnel, McCaffery concluded, his heart warmed by this welcome piece of Christmas news.

It is probably no surprise, then, to discover that Padre Pio has been prominent in Irish hearts at Christmastime as far back as the 1950s and beyond. In 1950s Ireland his name was everywhere to be seen and heard. Christmas programmes on Radio Éireann featured his story; radio reviews analysed books on his life; Padre Pio biographies were advertised as treasured Christmas presents; public lectures were held in various parts of the country.

Irish newspapers also reported how Italians celebrated the most sacred birth of all. They described how Rome had the most famous crib in the world, with 400 figures, how the church of Santa Maria in Via had moving figures and flowing water, and how the Adeste Fideles echoed from the choir lofts of the Eternal City's four great basilicas. But they never forgot the more modest, humble yet moving ceremony where Padre Pio blessed the crib at midnight in the isolated village of San Giovanni Rotondo. His was the most mystical midnight Mass of all.

THE LATER YEARS

1960 – 1968

The package tour revolutionised foreign travel in the 1960s. All-in, cut-price sun holidays, pilgrimages and honeymoon specials were on offer, most of them organised by Joe Walsh Tours. Throughout the decade, the company ferried thousands of Irish people to Rome and onwards to see Padre Pio. With employment booming and emigration falling, people had the money to pay for the new form of travel.

Inevitably, the bulk of the stories you are about to read come from people who went on these escorted tours. They were fortunate to attend Padre Pio's Masses, witness his stigmata and receive his blessings. Priests and journalists continued to travel, too. Although the friar was ageing fast, all who met him or saw him were left with indelible memories.

Dublin journalist Alan Bestic was one of Ireland's first visitors to San Giovanni Rotondo in the 1960s. He arrived at the friary in the early spring, just as the new decade was dawning.

The long, blue bus transporting Alan Bestic navigated its way through the hairpin bends and sheep-filled landscape on its journey from Foggia to San Giovanni Rotondo. The traditional mode of transport to the village had not changed one bit over the decades. The big difference was that the buses now travelled hourly, day after day, packed with pilgrims. Not even the sheep raised their heads as the buses' horns split the rural silence.

The bus reached San Giovanni in the early morning sunshine. Far below, the Adriatic winked in the dawn light. The first sight to greet the journalist was the new big white church built onto the old tiny church that had been replaced when it was no longer able to cater for the flood of pilgrims. On the left was the monastery. Inside it was Padre Pio, the man they had all come to see.

Bestic had arrived to witness Padre Pio's Mass and stigmata, which he did the following morning. At 4.30 a.m., the alarm went off. A chorus of alarms sounded in bedrooms all over San Giovanni at the same time. It was a dark, cold morning as the pilgrims and villagers set off up the hill to the church. The place was packed when he got there. He made his way to the sacristy, where he was being allowed to witness the friar robe for Mass. The atmosphere was muted, words spoken in low, reverential tones.

Suddenly, the door opened and Bestic was confronted by 'a stocky little monk.' It was Pio. 'He moved forward slowly, awkwardly. Those wounds in his feet are very real,' Bestic later wrote. 'Men fell on their knees and kissed his brown habit. He smiled faintly as they reached to kiss his stigmatised hand and almost diffidently he stretched it down to them. But all the time the sleeves of his habit hung low over those hands. Though he wore no gloves now, the stigmata remained carefully covered while he robed, clumsily. He is clumsy because the wounds in his hands are very real, too.'

The Mass had changed little over the decades. Despite the passage of time, it was still long, lasting almost an hour and a half. It was intense and moving. 'There were times when Pio seemed to be in a trance,' Bestic observed. 'He stood with his eyes closed, his hands clasped and he swayed slightly to and fro.

'Then slowly he raised his eyes to the altar, his face a strange mixture of suffering and joy. It was the face of a man in ecstasy. At that moment I felt deeply that the sturdy little monk was no longer with us. Beside me a cripple began to weep quietly.

'At last the long ceremony drew to a close. Padre Pio turned slowly to face the silent congregation. He raised his arms in final benediction and the sleeves slipped back from his hands. And there they were – the wounds. For a brief second we saw the stigmata.'

Following the Mass, Padre Pio walked back to the sacristy, where Alan Bestic watched him disrobe. Once again, pilgrims knelt and kissed his hands or sought his blessing. Others moved on to the confessional, where they sought forgiveness for their sins. As the future saint disappeared behind the confessional curtain, Bestic departed, heading out into the morning light.

This was 1960s San Giovanni and everything was changing. Looking down on the village, he could see a world of commerce coming to life. Souvenir shops, with their garish mementoes and picture books about Padre Pio, were readying for business. Cafés were opening; coffee stalls were preparing for their early-morning trade. A new dawn of commerce was rising over a village that had been transformed by the presence in its midst of a miracle-worker and living saint.

Following his return to England, Alan Bestic's assessment of Padre Pio appeared in the hugely-colourful, often-sensational magazine *Today*. The edition it was published in contained a feature on El Ingles, the bullfighter who had returned to his trade and whose 'courageous wife' sat and waited for his 'death in the afternoon.' There was also a story about 'a nymph-like blonde, who is a nightclub photographer' and advice on how to make your car 'absolutely theft-proof.'

Although the magazine has long gone out of business, its coverage of Padre Pio shows just how popular the friar and his stigmata had become by the turn of the 1960s. Bestic's article was the main feature in the Easter edition, and it was prominently advertised and heavily promoted. But then again, it concerned an extraordinary story and was written by a fine Irish journalist who clearly loved his trade. Like Padre Pio, Alan Bestic, too, would live well into old age, dying aged 92 in 2014.

Catherine Maguire, from County Cavan, travelled on one of the earliest commercial package tours leaving Ireland for San Giovanni Rotondo. It departed in 1962.

On Sunday, 14 October 1962, one of Joe Walsh Tours' special pilgrimages to Padre Pio departed from Dublin Airport. Since its establishment the year before, the tour company had been bringing Irish people on trips to Lourdes, Fatima, the Holy Land and Rome, including San Giovanni Rotondo. It can be confidently said that the company not only transformed the pilgrimage market in Ireland, but it introduced Irish people to low-cost, escorted package travel the likes of which they had never seen before.

The tour in October 1962 cost 66 guineas, included a stay in Rome and was 'escorted by a personal friend of Padre Pio.' The flight was by Aer Lingus Viscount, with its Rolls-Royce engines, representing the latest in comfortable prop travel. So well-regarded was the Aer Lingus Viscount that a *Kerryman* journalist wrote in 1962 of 'a perfect take-off, a smooth, comfortable journey with food and service of the highest standard and punctuality plus.' As passengers stepped from the aircraft, the journalist said, 'we were proud to be Irish and to travel in an Irish airline.'

Catherine Maguire, from County Cavan, was aboard that 1962 Joe Walsh Tours flight. 'I had read a book about Padre Pio and I wanted the privilege to be there at his Mass,' she told me. The cost, at 66 guineas, she added, 'was an awful lot of money because salaries were so small at the time. We shared the plane with other passengers who were only going to Rome. It was a long trip. We flew from Dublin to Brussels and then to Rome. We had to stop off in Brussels, I believe. We came down for refuelling.

'It was the first time they took people there (to San Giovanni) by bus from Rome. They always went by train previous to that. The bus driver, who was Italian, lost his way. There were about 30 or 40 of us on the bus. He hadn't an idea where we were. We were lost up the mountains and it was two o'clock in the morning before we arrived. He got into a lot of trouble getting us there, although he was alright coming back.

'Italy was very poor then. It wasn't that long after the war; it was ravaged. There weren't so many houses or hotels around. Nobody could speak English; now quite a number can. We stayed in the only hotel there at the time. Things were pretty primitive. The place was very nice but the food wasn't the best. The food was so different. We wouldn't even have seen spaghetti in Ireland back in those days. But the weather was beautiful.'

By 1962, air tours, bus tours and tourists arriving by train, taxi and private car were flooding into San Giovanni Rotondo to witness Padre Pio. Their primary focus was his five a.m. Mass. Catherine arrived there promptly at 4.30 a.m., and she went every day. 'The Mass was something else,' she recollected. 'The crowds were huge. The villagers were there from about two o'clock or three o'clock in the morning, standing outside to get in. I was there from about a half an hour beforehand. He was so prayerful at the Mass, it was lovely.'

By the early 1960s, resentment towards tourists travelling from various parts of Italy, not to mention from other countries, had become even more pronounced among the local population. Although aware of the hostility and discontent, Padre Pio was happy to meet with the latest Irish visitors and give them his blessing.

'It was very hard to meet him even then,' Catherine recalled. 'The natives wouldn't like you getting close to him. He called around one day to see us. He came in and blessed us in a little place near the convent. We all knelt down. He was very frail at that time. He had the wounds and there was somebody always helping him around. Unfortunately, the natives were banging on the door and created an awful fuss. They didn't want outsiders to be there at all. I didn't want to be fussing to get over near to him. Anyway, he didn't stay long.'

In the decades following 1962, Joe Walsh Tours became a colossus of the Irish overseas travel business. From their modest beginnings in 1961, by 1988 the company was sending over 100,000 holidaymakers to many exotic destinations, including 13,000 who went on pilgrimages. They organised 50 separate tour groups for the canonisation of Padre Pio in 2002, having already sent numerous tours to his beatification in 1999. By then, however, jet travel had overtaken the prop travel of the early 1960s, and the Viscounts were long gone.

Things had also changed in San Giovanni Rotondo. 'A lot of people who travelled in the old days would have been from the country and they were very comfortable with the old San Giovanni, which was old world,' Nuala Brady, former Italian pilgrimage manager for Joe Walsh Tours, told me. 'It felt like going to a little old country town. That was quite comfortable for a lot of people. But it has got very commercial now.

'It also was much more religious and there was a lot more praying. In those days they would probably have said the rosary on the flight going over. The priest would have been allowed to speak on the microphone on the aircraft, which wouldn't be allowed at all now.'

Things didn't change much, however, for Catherine Maguire who, despite the transformation of San Giovanni and the new means of travel, retained her devotion to Padre Pio. 'I spent five days in San Giovanni, I think, on that first trip,' she said, when concluding her interview. 'It was a long time, but San Giovanni was nicer and certainly a more real place at that time. I then went every year in the 1960s except for the year he died. I was devoted to him then all my life.'

Padre Pio's blessings were greatly cherished; so also were opportunities to kiss his wounded hands. Tom Cooney, from County Clare, was fortunate to experience both.

There was something very special about being blessed by Padre Pio. Apart from his holiness, there was the direct connection between his stigmatised hands and the hands of Christ on the cross. There were also the many miracles and graces connected with Padre Pio's blessings in the past. His invocations of favours from above – a good definition of a blessing – were much sought after and highly treasured.

Thousands flocked to his Masses and confessions to receive his blessings. Men queued in the sacristy to be granted them. Women, who weren't allowed into the sacristy, sought them elsewhere, either in the grounds or the chapel. How many times the friar invoked God or his mother to help people in trouble is anyone's guess, but we can be sure the number is high.

Tom Cooney, from County Clare, was one of those people who received Padre Pio's blessing. He waited for it along with 27 other men in the monastery. It was 'men only,' he was told, in keeping with the rule of the friary. The men waited nervously, their voices subdued, each one hoping that he might be singled out by the friar. An atmosphere of anticipation preceded the event.

An advance group of assistants informed the 28 men what to expect. 'We were told, "We don't know what he will do,"' Tom Cooney explained. '"He may walk in, bless you and walk on, we don't know. He will definitely bless you but he may or may not also give the wounded hand to someone to kiss. We want to have everyone ready for this because it could be any of you." They told us then, "Stand up until he comes in, when he comes in kneel down, take your rosaries and have them on your arm, medals in your hand and be perfectly still while he is with you."

'We waited for about ten minutes. Three or four Capuchin priests came in to where we were. We then heard the lift. Two monks, two Capuchin friars, linked him in. He was talking to them. He was dressed as a Capuchin friar. His hair was grey, as you'd see in the photos, magazines and books now. He couldn't speak English but he understood it and he said nothing to us.

'He stayed with us for about eight to ten minutes. He just looked around and had a look at us all for a couple of seconds, then returned again to talking away to his Capuchin friars for another few minutes. He turned around and gave another look. There was a great feeling of holiness there. He was a man that could read your mind and soul. Finally, they said, "Hold up everything and he'll bless everything you have." I held up rosaries and medals. Like any priest he blessed them and he blessed us all.

'Then he walked past each one of us. There was no ceremony. He just stood for a second before everyone, and everybody touched his habit. I was the only one he handed the wounded hand to, to kiss. I didn't say anything to him; I was just thanking God to be in the one room with him. I couldn't have asked for more.'

Perhaps the most remarkable story concerning a Padre Pio blessing took place in 1947. It involved a Sicilian girl named Gemma Di Giorgi, who was born without pupils in her eyes. Doctors told her distraught parents she would never have the power of sight. Their prognosis proved to be accurate and she was blind up to the age of seven. It was then that her grandmother intervened.

A devotee of Padre Pio, her grandmother decided to bring Gemma to San Giovanni Rotondo. At the end of Mass, the stigmatist approached the young girl, both unexpectedly and unprompted, and suggested that she receive her First Holy Communion. This she did, after first having her confession heard by Padre Pio. He then stroked her two eyes and said, 'May the Madonna bless you, Gemma. Be a good girl.' She immediately regained her sight. Her case mystified medical experts, as she saw without pupils for the rest of her life. It was one of those cases where an 'impossible' cure had occurred in defiance of medical science.

Another story concerned a 24-year-old Italian woman from Bologna, Giuseppina Marchetti, who broke her right arm. The event was a tragedy for her as she had undergone surgery on the same arm after an accident three years before. A second operation resulted in the joint being fixated, or frozen, in a locked position. She was told she would never have the use of her arm again.

She was blessed by Padre Pio in 1930, having travelled to San Giovanni with her father. The friar told her, 'Have faith in the Lord. The arm will heal.' Not long after returning home, she experienced the scent of roses. On the same day, her arm completely healed. Similar to the last story, the medical evidence was baffling – an X-ray revealed that both cartilage and bone in the arm were restored.

Examples of miracles, revivals or other transformations that followed blessings by Padre Pio are too numerous to mention in this book, or perhaps even in any book. No particular medical miracle followed Tom Cooney's blessing, and none was sought or required. The event, however, did change his life.

In the following years, the Clare man organised numerous pilgrimages to San Giovanni Rotondo and blessed thousands of people in Ireland with relics of the future saint. His most treasured relic – a Padre Pio mitten given to him in 1968 by Fr. Alessio, one of the friar's close friends and assistants – he eventually donated to Killaloe Church, where it is on permanent display. Above all, however, he never forgot that day in 1965 when he was blessed by Padre Pio and kissed his wounded hand.

'I just thought it was wonderful to be in the one room with him,' Tom concluded. 'It was the very same as if one was above in heaven. It was great to meet him in person, to be blessed by him and to kiss his hand. It was a great honour. He was an amazing man. I really couldn't have asked for more.'

Fr. Adrian Lyons, a Franciscan priest who was born close to Listowel, County Kerry, paid a visit to San Giovanni Rotondo in the early 1960s.

On his visit to the friary at San Giovanni, Fr. Adrian Lyons slept in a cell three doors down the corridor from the cell occupied by Padre Pio. To anyone who knew the story of the future saint, it was a questionable – if not terrifying – honour. After all, the stigmatic's cell was the reputed battleground between the friar and the devil on many occasions in the past.

Fr. Lyons must have been aware of Padre Pio's reports of hellish noises, violent beatings, cuts and bruises, indecorous language, blood-spattered bed clothing – all the consequence of battles with the devil and all conducted at night in the confines of his private cell.

'The ogre won't admit defeat,' Padre Pio once wrote to his spiritual director. 'He has appeared in almost every form. For the past few days he has paid me visits along with some of his satellites armed with clubs and iron weapons and, what is worse, in their own form as devils. I cannot tell you how many times he has thrown me out of bed, and dragged me around the room.'

From his subsequent report of his visit to San Giovanni – written in a biography that has all but disappeared, which was serialised in *The Kerryman* – Fr. Lyons seems to have escaped any hellish drama involving Padre Pio and the devil. On his first night there he did, however, awaken at four o'clock but only to the sound of his alarm clock. He had set it to ensure he would be ready for Padre Pio's five o'clock Mass, which he had been asked to serve.

His descriptions of the Mass are interesting to read. He first outlined how he headed down to the sacristy, shortly after four o'clock, expecting to see Padre Pio deep in prayer, with the rest of the church deserted. Instead, he encountered a teeming mass of people in the church, with at least 100 men cramming the sacristy. The men were lining up to have their names entered for confession with Padre Pio. If they were lucky, it might be possible today; if not, it might take weeks.

Fr. Lyons served at the Mass, gaining a bird's eye view of the extraordinary event. The huge crowd, once in the church, lost all sense of decorum, he said: 'In the rush for a good vantage point near the altar, one could almost say that it is a question of the survival of the fittest.' Some pray as they wait; others chat among themselves as if they were in the square outside.

Suddenly, Padre Pio enters and approaches the altar: 'Because of his wounded feet, he walks, or rather shuffles along slowly, and with rather obvious pain. There is now a death-like silence. All eyes are riveted on him. For the most part, they are eyes full of admiration and awe, but there are some of criticism and sheer curiosity. The reaction of that congregation is something of a study.'

Fr. Lyons gives a vivid account of the padre's features: 'I had expected to see an ascetical and gaunt looking man. On the contrary, he was stocky and vigorous, medium in height, somewhat rustic looking, with greying hair and beard. And those penetrating eyes! They seemed to look into the depths of one's soul, to read one's thoughts. I felt that they could be compassionate if needed, but, somehow, they struck me as being capable of striking terror into the most hardened heart where rebuke would be required. They were eyes into which I would not care to stare or gaze at for very long.'

The Kerry priest, who is close to the altar, also witnesses the padre's stigmatised hands: 'He tries to conceal them as much as possible. Naturally, those on the hands are the most difficult. For this reason he always wears mittens, except when offering Mass. And even here he takes precautions by wearing an alb with exceptionally long sleeves, with red embroidery on the extremities. Incidentally, it is only during his Mass that the ordinary person may catch a fleeting glance of those bleeding hands, and this provided one's position is close to the altar.'

The Mass itself is extraordinary, out of this world: 'Once Padre Pio begins his Mass, one's mind and thoughts seem to be taken out of and above the realms of this world and into a purely spiritual one. That peace of God, made possible by Christ's sacrifice on Calvary, seems to permeate the whole atmosphere. He himself seems to be as a man transformed or transfigured. One feels that something stupendous has begun, that a most sacred drama is being enacted.'

It was said of St. Francis that he did not appear to pray but to be a living prayer. This, too, is how Fr. Lyons felt about Pio's

Mass: 'All the movements are slow, recollected and devotional. There are very long pauses. What is passing through his mind? Presumably concentration on the great mystery. If those wounds which he bears reminds him at all times of Christ's passion, how much more so during the Mass wherein Christ is dying mystically, renewing the sacrifice of Calvary in an unbloody manner?

'At times, he seems agitated, as if he were looking out over a world laden down with sin and misery. At times, tears course down his cheeks. One is brought face to face, as it were, with the Christ of Gethsemane, of Calvary. Again one notices the lips moving as if in intimate colloquy with Christ.'

The Mass lasts for over an hour but no one gets tired, bored or restless. 'Occasionally, somebody close by can be heard sobbing quietly. Is it a sob of gratitude, or of repentance perhaps?' Fr. Lyons asks. The Mass over, Padre Pio descends from the altar and kneels for the after-Mass prayers. Unobtrusively, he is handed the mittens which, discarded during Mass, he puts on again. Few notice the discreet action. He then departs the altar.

Following the Mass, Fr. Lyons summarised his views of the stigmatic who, at the time, was aged 73 and who had only recently recovered from pleurisy: 'My first impressions were: what a martyr's life! The pain of those wounds, the complete absence of privacy even before his Mass, the rudely staring crowds. How any man could lead a life of prayer, keep humble and sane amidst all this! Rightly or wrongly, he struck me as being genuine.'

Following his visit to San Giovanni Rotondo, Fr. Adrian Lyons returned to Ireland to write his book on Padre Pio and publish his many excellent articles. He went on to publish other works, including *The Golden Sayings of Pope John XXIII*, adding to further books he had published years before.

He continued to serve as a priest, leading pilgrimages to San Giovanni, conducting missions throughout Ireland and running enclosed retreats. He died in 1987, leaving behind memories, particularly in County Kerry, of a man who knelt at the feet of Padre Pio, saw his wounds at first hand, and carried his message to the outside world.

The first Irish miracle attributed to Padre Pio came to light following a visit to San Giovanni Rotondo by Mona Hanafin, from County Tipperary, who sought a cure for her cancer.

In 1964, Mona Hanafin travelled to San Giovanni Rotondo with one aim in mind – to save her life. She was seriously ill with cancer at the time. A long series of hospital stays and medical interventions had failed to resolve her problem, and time was running out. With a major operation pending, Mona decided to place her life in the hands of Padre Pio hoping for nothing less than a miracle.

'In 1963 I went to San Giovanni for the first time,' Mona told me. 'The following year I was very, very ill with cancer. I was in my mid-20s. I was in and out of hospital and I wasn't getting any better. I lost an awful lot of weight and eventually the doctor said to me that he would have to remove my womb altogether and it would have to be done immediately. I said to him, "I'm going to Padre Pio and he will cure me." I left all my tablets at home and my mother and I went off to see Padre Pio.'

That journey in 1964 wasn't an easy one for Mona Hanafin. 'I was very ill on the streets in Rome,' she said. 'I had been very ill like that all the time, with constant vomiting and the likes.' From Rome, both mother and daughter made it to San Giovanni, where their first port of call was Padre Pio's five a.m. Mass. It was an early start for someone so unwell, not helped by the fact that her mother misread the clock and woke her at 1.40 a.m.

'We waited at the doors of the church until they opened at about a quarter to five,' Mona recalled. 'Then there was a rush in the door. The Italian people thought he was their own. During the winter they had him all to themselves; there was nobody else around. Here was my mother and I coming in and taking their places. They were very protective of him, and rightly so.

'We decided that I had to get near Padre Pio. We got into the church within two pews of where he was so I saw him very, very clearly during the Mass. I saw the stigmata when he removed the glove during the consecration. He turned around and he blessed everybody. I was with a group of other people and when I came out I said, "Padre Pio was looking straight at me." They said, "No, he was looking straight at us." In one glance he encompassed the whole church.'

Mona and her mother attended Mass every morning after that; in truth, they went everywhere Padre Pio was, always wishing to be in his presence: 'He said the Angelus at twelve o'clock from the gallery in the old church where he got the stigmata, where we joined him in prayer. In the afternoons he would pray up in the gallery of the new church. We'd all go and pray downstairs and be looking up at him. At night-time we all went around to the side to say goodnight to him. He had a handkerchief which he would wave and we'd wave handkerchiefs back.'

Mona's great hope was to get close to, and be blessed by, Padre Pio. Her chance came when the group she was with had an audience with the friar in the old church. She remembers the event well. 'When we came in, we came from the sunshine into the darkness and we couldn't see down to the confessional until our eyes were adjusted,' she recollected. 'We were all wondering where Padre Pio was. I looked down and, as the confessional was open to view, the next thing was that I saw him and he was looking up. I said to Mammy, "He is looking up at me."

'We were all lined up on either side of the pews and I was at the altar rails. Padre Pio was going to pass up through us all. The custom was that he would give you his hand and you would kiss it. That was the Italian custom. But I had read in a book that Padre Pio could see into your soul and I said, "I don't believe I'll be good enough to do that." I was looking at him and saying in my mind, "If you think I'm good enough would you put your hand on my head and bless me." He did. When he walked up and came to me he put his hand on my head and he blessed me.'

There was no instant cure for Mona Hanafin, no immediate transformation, no sudden relief from her symptoms. Instead, she remained acutely unwell and was lucky to make it home. 'I was very ill coming back on the plane and I was brought straight out to the hospital,' she recalled. 'Mammy said to the doctor, "My daughter is not well at all." He said, "Get her checked into one of the hospitals in Dublin."

'I became unconscious and I remained that way for two or three days or more. My temperature was 106.5. They gave me the last rites. I actually had gone so far that I could see myself from outside. I was looking down at myself and I could name who was around the bed. They sent for my family and my husband. They said, "She won't pull through."'

Contrary to all expectations, Mona did pull through. Not only that, but when she revived her problem was resolved and the cancer was gone. Her doctor was baffled and could offer no explanation. An operation, he said, was no longer necessary. At the time of writing, it is well over half a century later and the cancer has never come back.

Perhaps understandably, in the years that followed, Mona Hanafin became a devotee of Padre Pio and promoted his cause in Ireland. Her list of accomplishments on his behalf is far too long to enumerate in this book, other than to say that few Irish people contributed more to fostering devotion to the friar while leading innumerable groups to San Giovanni Rotondo both before and after he became a saint.

'I expected that he would be like a film star, such a wonderful man coming out on the altar,' Mona said, looking back. 'But when I saw him coming out, trying to walk and with the priests holding onto him, I just knew he was a saint. His shoe size was a size eight but his feet were so swollen with the blood that they looked like a size twelve. He had a wonderful presence about him. It wasn't a "show" presence; it was a "humility" presence of pain and prayer and gentleness. You knew as soon as you saw him that he was a saint.

'At the consecration you felt that he was talking to Jesus. They say that he was talking to Jesus and that the Lord would give him souls to take care of. One day he said how wonderful it was that Our Lady had accompanied him on to the altar. Seemingly, she did that nearly every day. You'd know by his eyes that he was looking not at the host but at something way beyond that. His eyes were aglow and glazed over as he was concentrating on the host. You knew it wasn't the host but that there was somebody there.

'Following his death he was such a loss. His whole life was dedicated to saving souls. He was a tireless confessor. You had St. Francis and St. Anthony but in our times of trouble you had Padre Pio. He was special, he was just sent to us for our time. And why did he do it? He didn't do it for himself; he did it for us, for mankind. I definitely regard him as the greatest mystic ever.'

The arrival of the miniskirt in the mid-1960s distressed Padre Pio. The following contains stories to that effect which are related by two people with strong Irish roots.

Few issues from the 1960s raised people's temperatures more than the miniskirt. Perhaps only Beatle haircuts and general long hair matched the level of outrage and disapproval generated by the new fashion trend. From its inception in the mid-1960s by Mary Quant – who famously named it after her favourite car, the Mini Cooper – to its demise at the end of the decade, the evils of the miniskirt were preached from pulpits, written about in newspaper editorials and even occupied the minds of theologians and psychologists.

Wearers of miniskirts were immoral 'rag-dolls,' one Dublin newspaper letter-writer remarked. A judge in Limerick banned them from his court. An unfortunate motorcyclist was fined five shillings in Dublin for carrying a pillion passenger side-saddle, even though, he said, he had to do it because she was wearing 'one of those short skirts.'

The arrival of Twiggy for a fashion show in Dublin, in 1966, raised the temperature even further when she declared, 'I like very short miniskirts.' Things were getting out of hand. 'Reading the newspapers one would be justified in thinking that we'll all have to be physically, or lawfully, restrained from wearing them,' a columnist wrote in *The Irish Press* in 1966. Even Radio Éireann felt obliged to get in on the act, broadcasting a lecture on the miniskirt after one of its main lunchtime news bulletins in February 1967.

Women who were young and not so young wore these new high-hemmed skirts and dresses on their 1960s visits to see Padre Pio in San Giovanni Rotondo. He hated these abominations, deeming them to be indecent, immoral and inappropriate. He would eject women from his confessional if they turned up in them, or if they arrived in tight skirts or wearing dresses with plunging necklines. He would mostly send the women packing before they entered the confession box; other times, if they made it inside, he would shout at them brusquely, 'Out! Out!'

He was so opposed to the new fashion that a message was posted on the church door as follows: 'By Padre Pio's explicit wish, women must enter his confessional wearing skirts at least eight inches below the knee.' The message also referred to an occasion where a woman tried to change her skirt before entering the box. It said: 'It is forbidden to borrow longer dresses in church and to wear them for the confessional.'

The background to that latter rule was outlined by County Donegal resident John McCaffery in his book *The Friar of San Giovanni: Tales of Padre Pio*. It appears that a woman who realised her dress was too short, and didn't wish to face thunderbolts from Padre Pio, borrowed a longer one from her friend before going to confession. She changed into it in the church. On entering the box, the friar opened the shutter, glared at the woman, and said, 'Well, have we been dressing up for carnival, then?' He immediately snapped the shutter closed.

Padre Pio additionally hated women's slacks and pant suits. One person who met him in the early 1960s was the Canadian author and one of his 'spiritual daughters', Anne McGinn Cillis, whose maternal grandfather came from County Kerry. She described encountering, during her visit, a fellow Canadian with an Italian background who could speak Italian fluently.

During her confession with the friar, he elicited that she sold pant suits and slacks from her clothes shop in Vancouver. He refused her absolution.

He proposed that the woman should return home to Canada and get rid of her accumulated stock of these items, but not by selling them to women. If she so wished, she could then return to San Giovanni where he would absolve her of her sins. Alternatively, she could seek absolution in Canada, but he would know whether she had, or had not, carried out his instructions. According to McGinn Cillis, the woman did as she was told and got rid of her stock.

He also hated clear, see-through nylons, demanding that his spiritual daughters wore designs of an opaque variety. Women's arms had to be covered; so did their heads. Men, including children, were obliged to wear long trousers; not doing so could result in a severe tongue-lashing. The emphasis was on conservative, sober, modest – you might even say 'old fashioned' – clothes.

Of course, Padre Pio wasn't alone among churchmen in his abhorrence of the new fashion trends. One noted theologian, Monsignor Lambruschini, said that the Catholic Church 'cannot approve the miniskirt.' He continued: 'Some brainless women, professing a pseudo non-conformism, end up resembling monkeys in adopting the most capricious excesses of fashion.'

The mandarins in the Vatican took a more sober line but effectively reached the same conclusion – they barred women in miniskirts from St. Peter's, the Vatican museums and the Sistine Chapel. Police stopped women whose hems were well above the knee. For a brief moment, however, it seemed that the Vatican had relented, when in May 1967 the actress Claudia Cardinale was admitted to a papal audience wearing a black miniskirt.

Hopes were dashed when the Vatican's daily newspaper, *L'Osservatore Romano*, speedily announced that the pope had not foreseen that any of his guests would wear miniskirts, and the fact that some – including Cardinale – had done so did not imply approval or tolerance of the style. Dreams of a reprieve for the miniskirt had proved premature.

The truth is that, despite his extraordinary powers, Padre Pio was an ageing man in the 1960s, with old-fashioned views and intolerant of things he disliked. He was out of touch with the era he was growing old in – not only disapproving of the new fashions but also dismissing television as a worthless medium and never watching it either alone or with his fellow friars.

It was unfortunate that he was in his 70s when the 1960s revolution was storming through Europe, its tentacles reaching outcrops as isolated as San Giovanni Rotondo. Had he lived another few years, his mood might have changed. Soon, ankle-length dresses were back in fashion and the dreaded miniskirt was on the wane, no longer revealing 'what should remain hidden,' to quote the catechism, and no longer antagonising people like Padre Pio who had grown up in more sedate, conservative times.

Patricia Connolly, from County Roscommon, tells the story of her deceased husband Jim, from County Fermanagh, who once went to confession with Padre Pio and was told that he would die young.

When Jim Connolly visited Padre Pio in 1966, the news he received was more than depressing. He had once contemplated becoming a priest and was very religious. He was also fascinated by Padre Pio and regarded himself as a devotee. It all led to Jim's visit to San Giovanni Rotondo, where he was fortunate to have his confession heard by the stigmatic friar.

What happened at confession was most strange. Padre Pio told Jim, who was then aged 23, that he would die very young. The remark was direct and unequivocal – Jim would never reach middle age or old age; instead, he didn't have long to live. Padre Pio also placed his hand on Jim's head and blood was left stuck to his hair. He cut off that strand of hair and kept it in his pocket until the day he died.

Six years later, Jim and Patricia got married. The marriage took place in Italy, near San Giovanni, in the parish of Jim's friend Don Carlo Carino. Two years after that, the couple's son was born and they named him Pio Emmanuel. Obviously, even with the passage of time, Jim was still fascinated by all things related to the future saint. No doubt he was also perturbed by that strange prediction.

'When I first met Jim he told me all about Padre Pio,' his wife Patricia explained. 'He was really taken with him. He used to joke about religion and say about himself, "Look, I have lovely hands just like Padre Pio."'

Jim told Patricia about the confession and the disturbing prediction. She didn't know if he worried about it. He certainly didn't appear to, 'although he might have worried inwardly,' she remarked. She, herself, certainly wasn't worried, believing that no one dies that young. 'You think they're going to live until 70 or 80 years,' she said.

As far as past predictions of Padre Pio were concerned, the couple might have been wise to agonise over the friar's ominous words. His prophecies had the uncanny ability to be right. Many examples are recorded. On one occasion, he advised a highly-active, healthy priest, aged 52, to cut back on his schedule, warning him that his life was hanging by a thread. Even though the suggestion seemed preposterous at the time, the man died four months later from cancer.

On another occasion, he cautioned a young priest not to plan any further studies and instead focus on death. Given that the man was aged 26 and seemingly in good health, the notion that anything might be amiss seemed absurd. He died suddenly and unexpectedly less than three weeks later.

Even as far back as Padre Pio's childhood, there was evidence of his extraordinary sensory powers. A former friend described how one day the young Francesco was in a field with his father, who was trying to dig a well. The father's endeavours were proving to be unsuccessful. Identifying a different part of the field, Francesco advised his father to dig there. The father did so and soon discovered water, according to the woman, who was quoted in C. Bernard Ruffin's book *Padre Pio: The True Story*.

Much later on, during World War II, those predictive powers were evident once more. Fearing that the bombing of Genoa was imminent, a resident of the city asked Padre Pio if his house would be safe. The friar confirmed that the city would indeed be bombed, but that the man had nothing to fear. Although the city was eventually bombed to rubble, the man's house was the only one left standing in an area that had otherwise been completely razed to the ground.

Unfortunately, Padre Pio's prediction regarding Jim Connolly also turned out to be true. Although living in England at the time of the pending tragedy, he frequently returned to Ireland to play football. It was on one of those visits that misfortune struck. Aged 33, he was involved in a car accident and, although initially unconscious and on life support, he later died. The date and time of his death were extraordinary.

'He was quite a few weeks unconscious and he eventually died at the age of 33,' said Patricia, who was working in England and came over and back to visit him in hospital. 'He died on the very same day that Padre Pio died and at the same time. It was 23 September, in the early hours of the morning. His mother was with him. It is quite a serious matter; you wonder about it, it is very strange.'

Many years later, in 1997, Patricia travelled to San Giovanni Rotondo, reliving old memories and tying up emotional loose ends, it would seem. Had Jim lived, the couple would have been

25 years married at the time. She travelled with a group from Belfast and in the company of Jim's cousin.

'It was very emotional,' Patricia recollected. 'I just thought, "Wouldn't it be nice if Jim was here."' During that visit she met Fr. Alessio, who had looked after Padre Pio, and he signed a prayer book for her son. In the years to come, she also kept in touch with Jim's good friend Don Carlo Carino. And she knew that, had Jim lived, he would definitely have returned to San Giovanni.

'I think it's very uncanny what happened to Jim,' Patricia said at the conclusion of our interview. 'Sometimes I am a bit frightened to pray to Padre Pio thinking things might go wrong. I pray to him but sometimes not too seriously just in case things may not turn out the right way. You wonder why Jim was killed, why he died on the date he did. You wonder did Jim die for a good reason or a bad reason. I still think about it a lot.'

Patricia McLaughlin, whose voice became well-known on Irish radio in the 1970s and 1980s, visited Padre Pio many times in the 1960s.

Listeners to Radio Éireann back in the 1970s and 1980s will remember the rich, warm voice of Patricia McLaughlin and her work on behalf of Wireless for the Blind. Her campaign was also waged in newspapers, especially in their letter pages and classified advertising columns. 'Think of the blind,' she would write. 'Think of their courage in a world of darkness. Radio is their eyes. Thank God for your sight.' She would then advise where donations might be sent.

It was a hugely successful campaign, waged on behalf of the National Council for the Blind of Ireland. Although it came into existence in 1934, its momentum grew after Patricia took over, with over 1,000 radio sets being distributed each year. The crusade – for that is what it was – had such an impact that when it ended in the mid-1980s, people would write to their newspapers bemoaning her departure and wondering where she had gone.

What people didn't know was the depth of Patricia's devotion to Padre Pio and her many visits to San Giovanni Rotondo in the 1960s. Not only did she attend his Masses, but she met him and was blessed by him. She defended the friar from his critics and spoke about him to her family and friends. Fortunately, Patricia also wrote about Padre Pio, leaving us with a record of her memories.

Patricia McLaughlin was one of those resilient, determined, independent women who live rich lives and stand out in the eras they inhabit. A Dubliner, she initially worked in the Civil Service and as a broadcasting assistant in Radio Éireann. She also studied elocution and trained at the Abbey School of Acting under the esteemed dramatist and theatre producer Lennox Robinson.

She was soon heading overseas, first to Geneva where she worked with the United Nations, and then to war-torn Congo where she acted as secretary to the Supreme Commander of the U.N. Forces. 'At night it is thrilling to watch the red sunset on the Congo river and the fireflies glowing in the warm darkness. But when I think of the sun on the Donegal hills I indeed miss the wonderful changes in seasons at home,' she wrote in an article published by *The Irish Press*.

She later returned to Geneva, where she offered this acerbic description of the city: 'If you are a person who wants to completely forget home roots, the humour, kindness and sympathy shown you in Ireland, then Geneva is the place for you.' She next lived for a time in Rome, and even travelled to Russia during an era when such journeys were fraught. She eventually came home to Dublin and her high-profile role with Wireless for the Blind.

It was while in Rome that she travelled to San Giovanni Rotondo to satisfy her curiosity about Padre Pio. She made many trips – the first might have been from curiosity but the others were 'from love,' as she later put it. He was old at the time. 'I expected to see an emaciated man,' she remarked. 'Instead I saw an old monk, of robust build, with a beautiful ethereal face – the face of a man whose soul truly transcends the frightful suffering of his human body.'

Her description of the friar's Mass was graphic and moving. He arrived on the altar robed in white and gold, his face as white as his hair, his hands swathed in brown mittens 'to control the gouts of blood.' As he entered the altar, 'there was not one garrulous Italian whisper to break the overwhelming silence,' she wrote in *The Irish Press*.

'I was overcome by the greatest sorrow I have experienced in my whole life seeing this poor 80-year-old man supported till he reached a chair on which he sat throughout the whole Mass. His face was transfigured – a combination of joy and suffering.'

Patricia was reminded of the words of poet John Masefield: 'We nailed Him there, aloft between the two thieves in the bright air.' She was also reminded of Golgotha, that hill, otherwise known as Calvary, where Jesus was crucified: 'At the Consecration the poor helpless hands held the Sacred Host. Here was Golgotha brought home to each and every one of us as never before.'

Patricia returned to San Giovanni on a number of occasions, but could only attend the friar's Mass. 'After Mass Padre Pio heard confessions but I could not confess as I do not speak Italian,' she recalled. Nor could she enter the sacristy to receive his blessing as the honour was reserved for 'male members of the congregation' only. Then, one day, her luck changed.

Standing in the sun-flooded square of San Giovanni, she was approached by the tall American Capuchin, Brother Martin, who was one of the guardians of Padre Pio. 'You've been here quite a few times and yet you never ask in to see the padre. Why?' he wondered. She explained that she thought he had enough people pestering him without adding to it.

'Brother Martin and I talked for some time, and next morning he arranged that I should meet the stigmatist,' Patricia later wrote. 'I can scarcely recall what happened. All I was aware of was an ethereal suffering face. The fingers touched my head, and I knew I was especially blessed.'

Having returned home to Ireland, Patricia McLaughlin never forgot Padre Pio and always spoke of her great admiration for the future saint. She defended him against his detractors – on one occasion, following a Telefís Éireann profile of the friar, vigorously refuting allegations that had been voiced on the programme and arguing that similar allegations had never surfaced during her time in Italy. She received support in the press for her defence of the friar.

She lived in Dublin for the remainder of her years, and it was in that same city – the city of her birth – that she died in 2016. The time up to her death had been difficult, but no doubt she had called on the help of Padre Pio. After all, she had once written: 'I hope that when during life I am inclined to be resentful of the will of God I will remember the poor suffering face of Padre Pio, who drank His cup to the last, saying, "Thy will be done."'

Derry man Fr. Pius McLaughlin's confession with Padre Pio in 1967 changed his life. At the time, he was a Franciscan brother but was harbouring other ideas about the direction his future might take.

In the early summer of 1967, Pius McLaughlin travelled to San Giovanni Rotondo along with three Franciscan provincials who wished to visit the stigmatic friar. As a brother, his job was to look after the provincials, who had arrived for the general chapter of the order in Assisi. There was no better man for the job. After all, he had already lived in Italy for five years –

working for four of them as a tailor at the Irish Franciscan College in Rome – and was conversant with the Italian language and Italian ways.

Brother McLaughlin, as he was then known, had made the arrangements for the trip, booking the three provincials and himself into the friary at San Giovanni and arranging for them to attend Padre Pio's Mass. During their stay, the provincials decided to attend Pio's confessions. Pius McLaughlin decided he would attend, too. 'I suppose that was the experience that transformed my life forever,' he told me.

At that stage in his life, Padre Pio's confessions were nothing short of legendary. He would tell people their sins before they had a chance to speak. He would know when people were telling only partial truths. He would reveal to penitents details of their lives which would leave them flabbergasted and asking, 'How could he have known?'

He would refuse absolution to those he knew were insincere; he would even eject people from the confessional before they had a chance to speak, knowing that they were about to conduct a bad confession. There certainly was a danger in disclosing your sins to Padre Pio, whether you were a man whose confessions he heard in the sacristy, or a woman whose confessions he heard down in the church.

There were many extraordinary reports associated with Padre Pio's confessions. On one occasion, a priest from an area far from San Giovanni decided to attend the friar's confessions to see for himself how credible he was. The priest had been prompted to undertake the trip having listened to nuns in a convent discussing the stigmatic, with some of them extolling his virtues, others claiming he was a fraud. The priest decided to arrive in civilian clothes, so that he might look less conspicuous.

While waiting in the queue in the sacristy, where confessions were held openly, he noticed Padre Pio staring at him. The staring continued for some time, which puzzled the visiting priest as the friar didn't know him. Eventually, Pio beckoned the priest to approach him and said, 'Father, go and put on your habit and then come back and I will hear your confession.' The priest replied, 'It is unnecessary, Padre. I came in order to find out something and I have found out what I wanted to know.'

There were sad but redeeming stories, too. An old, poverty-stricken woman from San Giovanni, whose son had died, was so distraught that she turned against God and all she had once believed in. Although she had other sons, the one who died was the apple of her eye and she missed him intensely. She was heartbroken and unwell, so much so that a family member asked Padre Pio to pray for her.

One morning, the woman walked to the church, where she made her confession to Padre Pio. Given the proximity of the confession box to the rest of the church, and the fact that it was in effect only semi-private, her crying and sobbing could be heard by all those waiting in line. She eventually emerged, tired and weary, and a friend accompanied her home. She asked the friend to put her to bed and to call her children and say, 'Padre Pio has pardoned me.' Those were her last words; she died soon after.

It was stories like those that formed the backdrop to Brother McLaughlin's confession with Padre Pio in May 1967. 'I went in and I rattled off my confession,' he told me. 'As far as I remember, I hadn't very much to tell. Then there was a great silence. Nothing was happening and I was wondering was he there. He said to me, "You didn't say you were a Franciscan lay brother." I figured maybe he had seen the habit but there was nothing I had said that suggested that I was a religious and a Franciscan lay brother. That kind of shook me.

'He followed it up by saying, "Would you like to discuss your problem, and what are you going to do about it?" At that point I got very, very scared. I could feel myself breaking out into a sweat. I didn't know what to say. I said, "I don't have a problem." He said, "You do." I said, "I don't." He said, "You do, and would you like to talk about it?" All this was in Italian. I had fluent Italian.

'Then it dawned on me all of a sudden what he was talking about, which was that I had this notion that I would love to have been a priest. But I had no background educationally. I was a lay brother. It never had happened before that anyone went from that status to being a priest in the Irish province of the order. He just said to me, "I advise you to pray fervently, speak to your superior, humbly ask for permission, trust in God and leave the rest to him."

'That I did the following week when I went back to Assisi. I sat down with my provincial. He was shocked to hear me talk like this. He pointed out all these obstacles that were there. I outlined my desire. I said I understood about my background education, that it had never been done before. But I said, "I'm willing to take this step and trust in God." He said, "OK, let's see what we can do."'

The rest is history. Although there were many obstacles in Pius McLaughlin's path, they were eventually overcome. He was sent to America where he did all his studies. He did very well, ending up with a Masters degree. He was ordained a Franciscan priest in 1973, later spending a long spell with the Franciscans in Dublin and afterwards in Rossnowlagh, County Donegal.

'I suppose if I were to take anything out of that personally,' Fr. Pius McLaughlin concluded, 'I would say that what I have learned and tried to live would be that there is a providence of God at work all the time. Nothing happens by chance. There are no coincidences. The other thing I learned was never to be afraid to risk – the fear of failure and the fear of risk keep all of us from jumping in.' The third thing he learned, of course, was the extraordinary impact Padre Pio could have on one man's life. It was something Fr. Pius McLaughlin never forgot for the rest of his life.

The following is not only an insight to Padre Pio's interest in football, as told by one of his fellow friars, but there is also the story of a strange football prediction he made in 1965.

In a conversation with Fr. Ermelindo Di Capua – the Capuchin friar who spent three years working with Padre Pio and who was a frequent visitor to Ireland – the author of this book asked if the stigmatist had been interested in football. Given that Padre Pio was Italian, it was my presumption that somewhere along the way football must have entered his life. The answer was immediate and emphatic.

'He loved football,' Fr. Ermelindo declared, happy that he was dealing with a light topic and not some profound aspect of his former colleague's spiritual life. 'He liked Inter Milan, but his favourite team was Foggia. He always looked out for their results.' Although the speed of the response surprised me, on reflection the future saint's interest in sport – in his local team, Foggia, and one of the greatest teams in history, Inter Milan – was revealing.

In the mid-1960s, when Fr. Ermelindo worked with Padre Pio and knew him intimately, Foggia were competing in Serie A, the top Italian league. Inter Milan were in the same division and riding high at the time, winning league titles – Scudetti – European Cups and Intercontinental Cups. There were light years between the teams, with the few matches that took place between them like battles between David and Goliath. A story lies therein.

Inter Milan were managed by the legendary Helenio Herrera, the Argentine who steered Inter to three Serie A titles and two consecutive European Cups. Foggia were managed by Oronzo Pugliese, who would later coach Roma, Bologna and Fiorentina. Inevitably, the two managers and their teams faced each other in league matches – one of them taking place in Foggia, in the depths of winter, on 31 January 1965.

On the day prior to the match, Helenio Herrera brought some of his players with him on a visit to Padre Pio. We don't know who those players were, but we do know there were enormous stars to pick from – among them Sandro Mazzola, one of the greatest forwards and attacking midfielders in history who could score lots of goals, and Giacinto Facchetti, one of the best defenders of all time. The truth is that whoever was there from that 'Grande Inter' team would have been a shining star.

Before leaving the friary, Helenio Herrera jokingly pushed his luck and asked Padre Pio: 'Let us win tomorrow's game and also the championship.' It was the sort of remark the outgoing, confident Herrera often made. Joking apart, no doubt he was aware of the potential power of Padre Pio to intercede on Inter's behalf. He was also conscious that Foggia were no-hopers. The friar's response was immediate.

'You will not win in our home, but you will win the Scudetto,' Padre Pio responded, without any hesitation. We don't know the reaction of Herrera but he must have been amused at the thought of Foggia beating the giants, Inter Milan. The following day, Foggia went into a 2 – 0 lead, only for Inter to draw level. But then came the shock of the season – a third goal for Foggia, sending the packed stadium into raptures of delight.

In the wake of that shocking loss to Foggia, Inter Milan went on a sustained run and won the Scudetto, with Sandro Mazzola their leading scorer. They also won the European Cup, beating Portugal's Benfica, and the Intercontinental Cup, defeating the

Argentine side Independiente. It was one of the finest years in Inter's history.

Helped by their famous win, Foggia managed to avoid the drop; they also did so the following season, but the next season again they were relegated. Even now, all these decades later, their victory over Inter Milan in 1965 is still immortalised in Foggia's history books and the event is spoken about with reverence by the club's fans and on Italian TV.

On numerous occasions I have pondered over that discussion which I had with Fr. Ermelindo in Knock, and I have thought about the famous win by Foggia over Inter Milan. It was, of course, only one small prediction, but whatever the issue – be it foreseeing deaths or predicting the next pope – there certainly was something uncanny about Padre Pio's ability to know what came next.

Many stories are documented. One of them concerns an evening in 1936 when Padre Pio was in his room, in the company of three people. He suddenly dropped to his knees and requested that they join him in prayer. On being asked who they were praying for, he said it was for the king of England who would soon be dead. Later that night, around midnight, he asked another friar to pray with him for the king, who he remarked had just died. The following day, the death of King George V was announced. He had died around midnight.

An even more extraordinary story is told of how he predicted the death of one of the carabinieri assigned to protect him. Calling the man aside, he told him to go home because within eight days he would be dead. The man was traumatised and protested that he was feeling very well. Even the carabiniere's superiors believed there was nothing to fear and were reluctant to give the man leave to return to his family. Eventually, they relented and the man died eight days later.

It is no surprise, then, to discover that the world of sport – just like Helenio Herrera of Inter Milan – often turns to Padre Pio for inspiration and for support. Sport is full of rituals and superstitions. Religious beliefs are frequently brought into play. A good example is former Republic of Ireland, Chelsea and Blackburn Rovers star Damien Duff's decision to play with a Padre Pio medal or relic in his sock or his boot. Many other examples exist, as well.

One notable case concerns the talented Italian midfielder, Antonio Nocerino, who played in the 2000s most notably for Juventus, Palermo and Milan. He always insisted on wearing number 23 on his shirt, commemorating the date of Padre Pio's death, 23 September 1968. He became a star not only with the clubs he played for but with the Italian national team. No doubt he believed the saint helped him throughout his career.

Somewhere along the way, however, Helenio Herrera and his megastars at Inter Milan must have felt let down by the future saint. On reaching the European Cup final in 1967, they faced Glasgow Celtic in the decider on 25 May. That day, with four non-Catholics in the side, Celtic won 2 – 1. Mind you, it is safe to say that close to 100 per cent of the Celtic fans were Catholic, perhaps providing some solace to Padre Pio as he viewed the unexpected, crushing defeat of one of his favourite teams, Inter Milan!

John Delamere and his wife Kay met Padre Pio in San Giovanni Rotondo in 1967. They were on honeymoon in Italy at the time.

In 1967, John and Kay Delamere got married and went on their honeymoon to Cattolica, near Rimini, in Italy. They stayed in the Hotel Murex for a week. They then went to Rome, where they stayed in the Hotel Diana. After that, they travelled to Foggia by train and took a taxi to San Giovanni to see Padre Pio.

'I remember we had no place to stay in San Giovanni,' John recalls. 'We met a taxi driver – Matteo was his name – and he brought us down to a bed and breakfast and they took us in. My big memory was that I had no cigarettes and I had to walk up to the local *tabac* to buy some. I was caught in a massive thunderstorm. All the lights went out; the only way I could see my way was with the lightning.

'I eventually got back to our room, where Kay was under the bed, afraid for her life. All I had brought with me from Rome was one outfit and I was wringing wet. The lights were out and we had to use candles, with the risk of starting a fire. But what I will never forget was the rain; it was coming down like stair rods.'

John and Kay stayed in San Giovanni for two days, during which they met Padre Pio. 'The idea to meet him had come from Kay's sister, Mairead Doyle, who was a friend of his and a big devotee,' John remembers. 'She had been visiting him since the early 1950s. She led tours out to San Giovanni and she organised talks and film shows about Padre Pio all around Ireland. If anything went wrong, she'd always say, "Have a word with Padre Pio." She had huge faith in him and she felt we should meet him.

'We met Padre Pio as part of a small, semi-private audience. It took place in a little room, a sort of an annexe. There weren't many people there, maybe about ten in all. I remember he sort of shuffled in, as he was old and unwell at that stage. He was really shook and feeble. He had to be helped by two people, one holding each elbow.

'He was dressed in a long brown habit, with a bare head and the beard. He wore mittens on his hands. He still had the big brown eyes that really looked through you. We were kneeling down and he came over to me and put his hand on my head and blessed me. He also blessed everybody else, including Kay. He was only there for a few minutes and then he was gone.

'I was very moved by what had happened, dumbfounded really. Kay was thrilled. There had been an odour of sanctity about him. He had exuded charisma and personality. There was a great sense of peace about him. You felt he was so near to God.'

The Delameres also saw Padre Pio saying Masses in San Giovanni. 'I remember the church would be packed and he had to be helped out from the sacristy,' John said. 'But I particularly remember how the Italian women who arrived to the Masses would be pushing and shoving you if you were in a front seat or near the edge of a pew. They all wanted seats up near the top and I think they objected to tourists.'

John and Kay have many memories of their 1967 visit. They particularly treasure a comment Padre Pio made to Kay after he was told who they were and that they had just got married. A priest translated it into English and he had said, 'God bless you and the children that you will have.' They also recall seeing Padre Pio at prayer. Above all, though, they regard themselves as fortunate that they met, and were blessed by, the friar not long before he passed away.

'Padre Pio only lived for about a year after we were there and I never saw him alive again,' John reflects. 'I did go back on two more occasions, but he had died in 1968. Kay went out there every year after that up to 2013, and that was her last visit. Mairead Doyle went out there again, too, and she died in San Giovanni in 2002.

'I am now in my 80s and I am still devoted to Padre Pio. If anything ever goes wrong, I turn to him. Whenever I hear non-believers saying there's no God, I always say, "What about Padre Pio?" and it shuts them up. There certainly was something special about him. He is the living proof that there is something there. So I was privileged to meet him and it was very special for me to have seen him. I always think back on that event as one of the biggest in my life.'

The popular local politician from County Donegal, Christy 'Egg' Gallagher, had a visit from Padre Pio shortly before he died in a Dublin hospital in 1968.

Probably one of the best-known and most popular county councillors in the history of Donegal town was a man named Christy 'Egg' Gallagher. He got his nickname for a very good reason – he exported eggs and poultry from his premises in Bridge Street. It was a business he inherited from his father, who had died in middle age. He added the wholesale distribution of beers and ales, and coal importing, to the activities developed by his father.

Christy 'Egg' was a much-loved character and an admired political campaigner. It seemed as if he was forever on the local council and had also stood for national office on two occasions, polling well although never getting elected. For a man of such energy and enthusiasm, it came as a surprise to everyone in Donegal when they heard he had cancer.

Christy 'Egg' battled hard against the disease. He called on a special friend of his – Padre Pio – to help him through his struggle. He was also loaned a piece of bloodstained bandage which the stigmatic had worn on one of his hands. The bandage was sent from Donegal to St. Luke's Hospital, Dublin, where Christy was being treated. He was thrilled to receive it and, no doubt, it contributed to the seemingly unassailable good humour he exhibited in the weeks ahead.

One day, a lady from Donegal visited the patient and found him to be in unusually good mood. He asked her if she wished to hear an explanation for his cheerful demeanour. He went on to explain how, during the night, Padre Pio had come to him, conversed with him, and asked him if he wished to share in the sacrament of Holy Communion. This he did.

Padre Pio then went to leave him. But Christy 'Egg' – who was always generous to others and who never lost his political instincts – suggested to the friar that there was another Donegal man in the hospital who would undoubtedly like to see him, too. It wasn't for nothing that Christy was a poll-topper in local elections!

There was a very strange twist to the story when, later in the same day that Padre Pio had appeared to Christy, it was announced on the radio that the stigmatic of San Giovanni Rotondo had died. The date was 23 September 1968. The odd coincidence – or perhaps explanation for the visit – didn't go unnoticed by the patient, his family and others back in Donegal. It must have meant a lot to Christy 'Egg'.

Not long afterwards, Christy 'Egg' Gallagher passed away at St. Luke's Hospital, Dublin. Later, his body was brought back home for burial. The *Donegal Democrat* reported how a convoy of cars travelled more than 60 km to meet the hearse, crowds lined the route in Donegal, and business was brought to a standstill as the procession wound its way through the town.

It was an extraordinary funeral, 'the biggest ever seen in South-West Donegal,' according to the local newspaper. Two government ministers attended, as did four other TDs, along with numerous councillors, former colleagues, family and many friends. But Christy 'Egg' was elsewhere, no doubt enjoying the company of a saint who brought him such peace and contentment, especially in the final weeks of his life.

When Padre Pio was dying in September 1968, Irish pilgrims were visiting San Giovanni Rotondo. They were among the last to see him alive and the first to witness him in death.

A very weak, frail, clearly-unwell Padre Pio said his Mass on the morning of Sunday, 22 September 1968. The church was packed to the rafters, the normal crush of people swollen by delegates who had arrived to attend a convention of prayer groups. The friar had to be wheeled to the altar, where he seemed tired and distracted, barely able to remember what he was supposed to say or do. After Mass, he collapsed on his way back to his wheelchair and had to be supported by assistants.

The 81-year-old had been in bad shape all week, suffering from chest pain, shortness of breath and loss of appetite. He knew he hadn't long to live. Everyone who saw him that week also knew the end was near. 'He was very old and very frail,' said County Dublin woman Kay Thornton, who attended one of his final Masses. 'He was hardly able to move. He had to be helped onto the altar. He was sitting down during the Mass. He stumbled on the way back into the vestry and someone had to catch him.'

The rest of that Sunday was difficult for Padre Pio. He barely made it through the sacristy after Mass, looking pale, with glazed eyes. He was then helped to his room, where he was eventually examined by a doctor. He struggled a few times to wave to the crowd congregated beneath his window. They chanted back with warm affection, 'Viva! Viva! Viva!'

That evening, he reported seeing 'two mothers,' most likely referring to the two women who had dominated his life and who he had loved so dearly – the Blessed Virgin and his own mother, Mamma Peppa. A friar heard his last confession and he renewed his priestly vows, following which a very weak Padre Pio asked to be helped from his bed to an armchair. Then, at 2.30 a.m., on the morning of 23 September, the unthinkable happened. Surrounded by a small group of friars, Padre Pio uttered his last words, 'Jesus.....Mary.....Jesus.....Mary,' closed his eyes, took his last breath and died.

Although they could never have guessed that things would have turned out this way, an Irish tour party, consisting of 83 pilgrims, had been in San Giovanni during Padre Pio's final days. They had attended his Masses, received his blessing and been greeted individually by the friar. They had been among the last to do so. Another Irish party, organised by Clare man Tom Cooney, was packing its bags back in Ireland and would shortly be on its way.

The late Kay Thornton was with the Irish party who were present during the friar's last days. They were returning to Rome when the news of his death was announced. She came back to San Giovanni, travelling via Foggia on the overnight train.

'I was determined to go back, although most people stayed in Rome,' Kay reflected. 'I kissed him laid out in the coffin. It was unbelievable how many people were there. You couldn't move with the people. People were queuing night and day to pass the coffin. There were so many coming, and the doors had to be closed over for the funeral. The people nearly went crazy because they couldn't get in. It was very moving. It was very special to have been there.'

The town of San Giovanni Rotondo was awash with people in the days following Padre Pio's death. They travelled from all over Italy and abroad, adding to the numbers already there for the prayer-group convention. With the hotels filled to capacity, tents were erected to cater for those in need of shelter. Many slept in cars or buses. Extra police were called in, some of them assigned to protect Padre Pio's coffin from overzealous mourners who wished to kiss his remains.

By a strange quirk of fate, Cork woman Mary O'Connor, who we heard from earlier in this book, had arrived in San Giovanni a few hours before Padre Pio died. She was with her husband Dan and their children, along with some other young children, too. After a long flight and a tough road journey, they had reached their hotel at midnight only to be told that no booking existed. They got to bed very late.

'The next morning, we got news that Padre Pio had died during the night, a few hours after we had arrived,' Mary O'Connor recollected. 'The only thing I said was, "He's suffered so much and he's gone to heaven!" Dan said, "Let's get the children up and dress them and we'll go up to the church and see what's happening." When we got there, there were lots of policemen and they were putting up barriers. His Italian women followers were arriving already. I thought, "God! What are we in for?"

'Dan said, "We'll go up to the door of the church," which we did. We knew no Italian, but I said to the guard, "Padre Pio! Irlanda! Bambinos!" Believe it or not, he opened the door and let us in. Padre Pio's body was already there, in his coffin, up in the altar area. Dan handed two of the children who were with us to a policeman, who in turn passed them over to kiss Padre Pio. We wanted to have our own child kiss him, too. We took him to a priest and asked him would he lift him in where the coffin was, which he did.

'I then said to Dan, "Would you stay with the children? I want to get nearer to Padre Pio." I went to the back of the altar and I got in. As I got there, they were changing the candles on the coffin. I asked the priest, "Would you mind giving me one of the candles?" He gave one to me. Pieces of it have gone all over the world.'

On Thursday, 26 September 1968, 60,000 people lined the streets as the body of Padre Pio was borne through San Giovanni. The entire town closed down. Black-bordered flags flew at half mast. Hundreds of veiled women, dressed in black, knelt as the open hearse bearing the coffin passed by. The body was eventually placed in the crypt of the church of Santa Maria delle Grazie.

Although his physical remains were in the crypt, the real Padre Pio was gone. The challenge, he had once said, was not death but eternal salvation. Holiness meant 'living humbly, being disinterested, prudent, just, patient, kind, chaste, meek, diligent, carrying out one's duties for no other reason than that of pleasing God and receiving from Him alone the reward one deserves.' Even by those exacting standards, Padre Pio was far away, in the company of his two mothers in heaven.

ACKNOWLEDGEMENTS

The time comes when first-hand witness testimony is no longer available, forcing us to rely on recorded historical accounts. Fortunately, when it comes to Padre Pio, we are not at that stage yet. Although he was born a long time ago, in 1887, he died within our lifetime, in 1968. As a result, we can still acquire rich insights from those who met him, spoke to him, witnessed his priestly work or benefited from his miracles and cures.

I have included in this book a mixture of recent interviews, old interviews and updated interviews with people I encountered from 2007 to the present day. Some have passed away since I interviewed them, including wonderful women such as Kay Thornton and Mary O'Connor. Others are still in fine health and remain devoted to the saint.

By now, you have read their stories and are aware of their names. Rather than list each one again, let me thank them for providing me with their remarkable insights and personal accounts. It was a pleasure to see how much love and affection they still held for a man they met half a century, and more, ago.

Extensive research was needed regarding Padre Pio's pre-1950s – and even post-1960 – Irish encounters. Many newspapers proved indispensible, including old editions of *The Irish Press*,

The Sunday Press, *Irish Independent*, *Sunday Independent*, *The Cork Examiner*, *Evening Herald*, *The Irish Times*, *Belfast News Letter*, *L'Osservatore Romano*, *Il Giornale d'Italia*, *Il Tempo*, *The Irish Catholic* and, in particular, two local papers, *The Kerryman* and *Limerick Leader* both of which took a keen interest in the life of the saint and his devotees.

Other valuable insights were contained in the now-defunct *Ballina Herald* and *Derry People and Tirconaill News*, along with the still-thriving *Connacht Tribune*, *Munster Express*, *Ulster Herald*, *Nenagh Guardian*, *Fermanagh Herald*, *Mayo News*, *Anglo-Celt*, *Westmeath Examiner*, *Strabane Chronicle*, *Longford Leader*, *Donegal Democrat*, *Donegal News* and *Donegal Times*.

Of special importance were two editions, from 1960, of the long-disappeared *Today* magazine, which was published in the United Kingdom. My thanks also go to *The Daily Telegraph*, *Dublin Review*, *The Irish Digest* and *Commonweal* magazine. Anyone interested in that famous 1965 football match between Foggia and Inter Milan, which so enthused Padre Pio, can find it on YouTube should it still be there. Readers interested in the early economic conditions of the region around Foggia, San Giovanni and Cerignola will find some remarkable insights in Lucia Chiavola Birnbaum's *Black Madonnas: Feminism, Religion and Politics in Italy*.

The best book ever written on Padre Pio, by a mile, is C. Bernard Ruffin's *Padre Pio: The True Story*, which was first published in 1982 but is still available through various outlets. Other outstanding books include Fr. Charles Mortimer Carty's

Padre Pio: The Stigmatist, Malachy Gerard Carroll's *Padre Pio*, and John McCaffery's *The Friar of San Giovanni: Tales of Padre Pio*. All were most helpful in the process of putting this book together and come highly recommended.

Other important texts on the saint include Mary Ingoldsby's *Padre Pio: His Life and Mission*, Fr. Augustine McGregor's *Padre Pio: His Early Years*, Fr. Pascal Cataneo's *Padre Pio Gleanings*, and also Fr. Francesco Napolitano's *Padre Pio of Pietrelcina: A Brief Biography*. Additional compelling works include *Pray, Hope, and Don't Worry: True Stories of Padre Pio* by Diane Allen and *Padre Pio and America* by Frank M. Rega. Unfortunately, with a few exceptions, many of the books mentioned above are well past their publication dates and can be hard to find, although some can be bought in electronic form on the internet.

Rich nuggets of information can be found in other, often hidden, sources. Fr. P. Hamilton Pollock recounted his World War II odyssey in his engaging *Wings on the Cross*; Alec Randall provided similarly important information about Dr. Paschal Robinson in his book *Vatican Assignment*; while Seán Ó Faoláin's *South to Sicily* is not only beautifully written but provides vivid descriptions of the friar and San Giovanni Rotondo in the late 1940s. Maurice Harmon's biography *Sean O'Faolain: A Life* was also invaluable, as was *Priests* by Fr. Robert Nash, which was published in 1961.

Anyone interested in the life and times of Graham Greene, including his visit to San Giovanni, would be well advised to investigate Norman Sherry's definitive three-volume study *The*

Life of Graham Greene. Information on the author's visit to Padre Pio is also contained in a letter he sent to fellow-writer Kenneth L. Woodward, which was published in *The New York Review of Books* in 1990. Background information on Barbara Ward is contained in the thorough, comprehensive study by Jean Gartlan titled *Barbara Ward: Her Life and Letters*.

William 'Bill' Carrigan wrote about, and spoke extensively of, his wartime visits to Padre Pio. Two of his papers were particularly useful when compiling this book. The first is very simply titled *An Introduction to Padre Pio*; the second is called *U.S. Soldiers Attend Padre Pio Masses*. The eulogy delivered at the funeral of this wonderful man in November 2000 was also of crucial importance.

Cardinal Cormac Murphy-O'Connor's autobiography – *An English Spring* – was priceless concerning his visit to the famous friar but is also a rewarding and enjoyable read. I am likewise grateful to the Cistercian College Union's quarterly publication *Roscrea Review*, which contains an excellent report on the shock arrival of the future Pope Paul VI to the abbey in County Tipperary.

The Waterford Archaeological and Historical Society Journal was a rich source of insight and information for two stories connected to the city. In 1995, it featured a well-researched article titled Teresa Deevy, Playwright (1894 – 1963) by Martina Ann O'Doherty. A year later, in 1996, the journal contained another outstanding study, Maria Montessori – Her Links with Waterford, by Sr. M. Redemptoris Cummins and Sr. M. Josepha

Phelan. Both are excellent sources of information and provide a thorough background to their respective subjects.

As always, various individuals deserve thanks for the help or support they provided in the writing of this book. Jerry O'Sullivan, Ann Wilkinson, Charles Tindal, the O'Connor family from Cork, the late Fr. Ermelindo Di Capua, Mary Briody, Ann Kelliher, Patricia Comiskey and Brother Kevin Crowley from the Capuchin Day Centre for Homeless People require special singling out.

I am also indebted to Giuilia Adam, who provided help with some tricky Italian – English translations, and Pauline Dwan – sister of the late Patricia McLaughlin, who featured earlier in this book – for the background information she provided. The public libraries in both Cork and Waterford cities were most cooperative and obliging, as were Linda Monahan and Barbara Ryan of Typeform, who performed sterling work.

There are three other people deserving special praise. The first is Prof. Con Timon for his medical guidance and help, without which this book would never have been written. The second is Úna O'Hagan, whose support and advice were, as always, beyond compare. The third is Padre Pio, whose hands seemed to guide this book at every turn. The road he travelled was a difficult one, with a beautiful destination at its end. Let's hope this book, which followed its own difficult road, has brought those who have read it to a similar beautiful destination through the stories it contains.

ALSO FROM CAPEL ISLAND PRESS

THE DISTANT SHORE

MORE IRISH STORIES FROM THE EDGE OF DEATH

Colm Keane

The Distant Shore is packed with a wealth of new Irish stories about life after death.

Extraordinary accounts of what takes place when we die are featured throughout. Reunions with deceased relatives and friends, and encounters with a 'superior being', are included.

Visions of dead family members are vividly described. The book also examines astonishing premonitions of future events.

This compilation was inspired by the huge response to Colm Keane's number one bestseller Going Home – a groundbreaking book that remained a top seller for six months.

Containing new material and insights, The Distant Shore is indispensable reading for those who want to know what happens when we pass away.

Reviews of *The Distant Shore*

'Amazing new stories' *Irish Independent*

'Terrific, wonderful read' *Cork 103 FM*

'A source of genuine comfort to anyone who has suffered a bereavement' *Western People*

ALSO FROM CAPEL ISLAND PRESS

HEADING FOR THE LIGHT

THE 10 THINGS THAT HAPPEN WHEN YOU DIE

Colm Keane

This explosive book reveals the truth about what happens when we die.

The ten stages we go through when we die are outlined for the very first time. They establish conclusively that death is a warm, happy experience and is nothing to fear.

Based on five years of research, the author has drawn from the real-life stories of people who have temporarily died and returned to life.

This definitive book provides you with all you need to know about the stages of death as we head for the light.

Reviews of *Heading for the Light*

'Absolutely fascinating' *RTÉ One*
'Provides much pause for thought' *Sunday Independent*
'The mysteries of dying and death from those who know'
The Irish Catholic

Capel Island Press
Baile na nGall, Ring, Dungarvan,
County Waterford, Ireland
Email: capelislandpress@hotmail.com